Building English Vocabulary with Etymology from Latin
Book II

Peter R. Beaven

Building English Vocabulary with Etymology from Latin
Book II
Peter R. Beaven

Editor:
Katharine Webster

Contributors:
Nicia Gruener, Paulette Ghassibi
Stephen E. Stapczynski, Dominic M. Brown
S. James Boumil III, Nikhil Deliwala, Christian Waters

Revised August 27 2018

Published by
The Cheshire Press
an imprint of The Cheshire Group
Andover, MA 01810
www.cheshirepress.com

All rights reserved. No part of this book may be reproduced or transmitted in any form or by any means without the express written consent of the author, except for the inclusion of quotations in reviews.

Copyright © 2005-2008 by Beaven & Associates

ISBN: 978-0-9987465-1-7

Registration Number / Date TX0006858641 / 2007-08-20

Printed in the United States of America

Beaven & Associates
3 Dundee Park, #202 A
Andover, MA 01810
Tel.: 978 475-5487
www.beavenandassociates.com

Beaven, Peter R.
Building English Vocabulary with Etymology from Latin
Book II

Contents

Etymology in Building English Vocabulary..5

Lesson I
ac/acr, ag, act, agri/agrari, ali, alt, alti..7
Lesson II
amo/amor, amb/ambul, anim, annus/enn, aperio, apt..13
Lesson III
arm, art, aud/audit, aur, avuncular, basis, battuo, beatum..................................19
Lesson IV
belli, bibo, breve, cad/cas, calcitro, cand, canto..25
Lesson V
cap/cip, caput/capitis, carn, castigo, cerebrum, cern..31
Lesson VI
ced, celer, censeo..37
Lesson VII
cent, cid/cis, cit/cital, civi..43
Lesson VIII
clam, clar, claud, clavis..49

Test 1..55

Lesson IX
clin, clivus, cognit, collum, compl, copia, coquo, cord..59
Lesson X
corpor, cred/credit, cresc, cruc, cubo, culp, cupio..65
Lesson XI
curr/curs, da/dat, dent, dextra, divin, doc/doct...71
Lesson XII
dict, doleo, domin...77
Lesson XIII
domit, dormio, dorsum, duc/duct, ego, equ, err..83
Lesson XIV
fac/fic/fec/fect, facies, fari, fall/fals, ferv..89

Test 2..95

Lesson XV
fer/lat, festus, fid, fin..99
Lesson XVI
fingo/figuro, firm, flect/flex, flor, flu..105
Lesson XVII
fort-, fors/fort, forum, frag/fract, frater, frons, fug...111
Lesson XVIII
fus, gargo, gen/genere...117

Lesson XIX
glomus, grad/gress, grat, greg..123
Lesson XX
her/hes, impleo, incendo, ira, iter/itiner, ire..129

Test 3..136

Lesson XXI
jac/jec, jocus, judico, junct/jug, jut/jurat...140
Lesson XXII
labor, lateral, lavo/luo, leg, lego, lev..146
Lesson XXIII
liber/ libr, liber, licencia, ligo, lingua, literal, loc..............................152
Lesson XXIV
loqu/locut, luc/lum, ludo..158
Lesson XXV
man/manus, mar, mater/matr, medi...164
Lesson XXVI
mel, mem/min, mendum, mereo, merg/mers, min..............................170
Lesson XXVII
mit/miss, mob/mot/mov...176

Test 4..182

Appendix A

Quizzes..187
Quiz 1: Chapters 1-5..189
Quiz 2: Chapters 6-10..180
Quiz 3: Chapters 11-15..191
Quiz 4: Chapters 16-20..192
Quiz 5: Chapters 21-27..193

Answer Key...195

Index..205

Etymology in Building English Vocabulary

The word "etymology" refers to tracing the origin and historical development of words in a language. How is a given word derived from an earlier word or words in a native or foreign language?

Just as we can "parse" or break up a sentence into parts of speech - noun, verb, adjective, adverb, etc. - so we can deconstruct a given word into its constituent meaning elements and trace their origins. For example, the word "etymology" consists of an original Greek root "etymon" - meaning "an earlier form of the same word" - and the Greek "logos" - meaning "word" or "speech", which took on the later form "-ology" - meaning "study of." So, there we have the etymology of the word "etymology."

Studying the etymology of vocabulary words reveals repeated word-formation patterns, so that we can dissect or guess the meanings of unfamiliar words based on their constituent prefixes and roots that we have encountered earlier. For example, by knowing that the prefix "pre-" means "before" or "ahead" and that "dict" is rooted in "speaking" or "saying," we can surmise that "predict" means to foretell or talk about something before it happens.

The English language is built primarily from the Anglo-Saxon (Germanic), Latin, and Greek languages. Historically, the Angles and Saxons drove out the original Celtic inhabitants and occupied Britain, and after a few brief occupations by the Roman legions, in 1066 the tribes were defeated by the Norman leader William the Conqueror, who spoke French - a language derived almost entirely from Latin. Over time, the Germanic and Latinate languages blended to become what we know as English.

Because Latin is such a fundamental basis of English and because Latin is built from a regular system of "reusable" prefixes and roots, studying these elements makes learning vocabulary more efficient. Instead of learning word meanings in isolation, by learning a standard set of Latin prefixes and common roots we can "mix and match" to learn several new words or variations. The study of etymology thus can accelerate the expansion of our vocabulary while helping us appreciate how meanings and usages have evolved.

For example, knowing that the root "gress" means "step" or "advance", and knowing a series of prefixes, we can deduce word meanings:

Prefix	Meaning	Example
"ad"	= to, toward	address ("g" in "gress" becomes a "d")
"co, con"	= together	congress (movement together)
"di"	= split	digress (move away from)
"e, ex"	= out of, from	egress (way out, exit)
"in"	= in, into	ingress (way in, entrance)
"pro"	= forward, for	progress (move forward)
"re"	= back	regress (move backward)
"trans"	= across, over	transgress (move across)

So many of the words in English that relate to the intellect, words that make us pause to think and study, come from the Greek. The Roman conquest of Greece and admiration for its culture led to the incorporation of many Greek terms into Latin. So we make a point of studying Greek roots and prefixes as well. For example, the Greek root "pathos" means "feeling" or "suffering", from which come such words as:

"a"	= not	apathy (not caring)
"anti"	= against	antipathy (dislike or hostility)
"em, en"	= into, in	empathy (sharing in another's feeling)
"sym"	= together, with	sympathy (feeling sorrow for another)

In addition, there are other English words based on the same root, such as "pathetic", "pathology", "pathos", and so on.

Consider the common prefixes and cross-connections of the words below:

telecommute	micron	automaton	extrasensory	intercede
telegraph	micrograph	autobiography	extravehicular	intercept
telphone	microphone	automobile	extraterrestrial	interrupt
telescope	microscope	autograph	extraordinary	interdict
television	micromanage	autonomy	extralegal	intervene

or the roots "duc" ("lead"), "fer" ("bear, bring"), "port" ("carry") and "vers" ("turn") as below:

aqueduct	confer	report	converse
conduct	defer	deport	diverse
deduce	refer	transport	reverse
duct	transfer	teleport	adverse
ductile	prefer	airport	perverse
educate	offer	purport	obverse
induce		export	averse
produce		import	inverse
seduce		comport	transverse
viaduct		support	controversy

In the series Building English Vocabulary, a student discovers that from just one Latin or Greek root springs an exponential growth in his vocabulary, sharpened tools to articulate the written or spoken word. A broader knowledge of English leads him to greater ties to the shared cognates of French, Spanish, Italian, and Greek. A stronger grasp of English brings a deeper understanding of the plays of Shakespeare, the novels of Dickens, the essays of Emerson, the poetry of Emily Dickinson, or the oratory of Lincoln and Churchill., who as national leaders, marshaled the English language — the former to invoke peace — the latter to evoke resolve for impending battles, the victories of which in the post bellum of the twentieth century helped thrust English into its role as the lingua franca of the modern world.

Lesson I

ac/acr, ag, act, agri/agrari, ali, alt, alti

| *AC, ACR* | *AG, ACT* | *AGRI, AGRARI* |
| sharp | do | field |

| *ALI* | *ALT* | *ALTI* |
| another | other | high; deep |

*acerbity, acrid, acrimonious, acumen, acuity, acute, exacerbate
agility, agitate, agrarian, agriculture, alias, alien, alienate
alter, alteration, alternate, altruistic, altimeter, altitude*

Word Definitions

acerbity   **n.** sourness of taste, character, or tone
"The critic's biting, dismissive review was tinged with <u>acerbity</u>."
acerbic (adj.)
acerbus sour tasting; bitter; harsh

acrid   **adj.** unpleasantly bitter or pungent
"The <u>acrid</u> smoke made ours eyes water and throats burn."
acridity (n.)
acer, acri- sharp, pungent

acrimonious   **adj.** characterized by anger and bitterness
"Contested divorces can lead to <u>acrimonious</u> confrontations."
acrimony (n.)
acuere to sharpen; to become sour

acumen   **n.** the ability to make good judgments and decisions
"Bill Gates' luck and business <u>acumen</u> made him a billionaire."
acuere to sharpen

acuity   **n.** sharpness or keenness of thought, vision, or hearing
"A dog's auditory <u>acuity</u> far exceeds that of the human ear."
acuere to sharpen

acute	**adj.** perceptive, finely honed; (of a situation) dire, severe; (of a disease) of sudden onset and short duration "Migratory birds need an <u>acute</u> sense of direction." *acuere* to sharpen < *acus* needle
exacerbate	**v.** to make (something bad) worse "His displeasure was <u>exacerbated</u> by her further nasty remarks." *exacerbation (n.)* *exacerbare* to irritate, to enrage: *ex-* (expressing intensity) + *acerbare* to embitter, make sour
agility	**n.** the state or quality of being nimble "An Olympic gymnast's routines require great <u>agility</u>." *agile (adj.)* *agere* to do, to drive
agitate	**v.** to upset (someone) or make them nervous; to arouse public opinion (against established order); to shake vigorously "Although he knew the music annoyed Matt, Steve made it louder simply to <u>agitate</u> him." *agitation, agitator (n.)* *agere* to do; to drive; to urge
agrarian	**adj.** relating to cultivated land or agriculture **n.** a person who advocates a redistribution of landed property "Hunter-gatherers eventually settled into an <u>agrarian</u> way of life." *ager* field, farm
agriculture	**n.** the science or practice of farming (growing crops and raising animals) "<u>Agriculture</u> in the U.S. has shifted from small family farms to large, corporate agribusinesses." *ager* field + *cultura* growing, cultivation
alias	**n.** a false or assumed identity; (in computing) an alternative name or label that refers to a file, command, or address and used to locate or access it "William Bonney is better known by his <u>alias</u>, Billy the Kid." *alius* other, another, different
alien	**adj.** belonging to a foreign country; unfamiliar and distasteful **n.** a foreigner; being from another country or world "He found his surroundings <u>alien</u> when he first emigrated." *alius* other, another, different
alienate	**v.** to cause to feel isolated; estrange "His mean gossip <u>alienated</u> his friend and ended their relationship." *alienare* to estrange or lose possession < *alias* other, different
alter	**v.** to change in character, appearance, or composition; to adjust for a better fit; to spay a domestic animal "Global warming threatens to <u>alter</u> the climate for the worse." *alter* other

LESSON I AC/ACR, AG, ACT, AGRI/AGRARI, ALI, ALT, ALTI

alteration n. a change; a modification
"New requirements led to <u>alterations</u> to the original plan."
alter other

alternate v. to occur or to do in turn repeatedly; switch back and forth
n. substitute; person acting in place of another
adj. every other
"The boy was mad that the coach made him an <u>alternate</u>, not a starter."
alternare to do by turns < *alter* other

altruistic adj. selfless; acting without expectation of reward
"To donate a kidney anonymously is an <u>altruistic</u> act."
alteri huic for this other

altimeter n. an instrument used to determine altitude (in aircraft)
"The jet's <u>altimeter</u> showed it was cruising at 30,000 feet."
altus high

altitude n. the height of another object or point in relation to sea level or ground level
"As <u>altitude</u> climbs from sea level to mountaintop, the air thins."
altus high

Exercise A

Fill in the blanks in the sentences below with the correct form of a word in the scroll above.

1. Workers on site when the factory caught fire were hospitalized after the burning chemicals produced an _____ smoke that nauseated them.

2. The Rhode Island night club was already a fire-trap, but the band's use of pyrotechnics _____ the danger.

3. Superman's _____ is Clark Kent.

4. Although her _____ and strength were unmatched, it was Keri Strugg's personality that captured America.

5. J.D. Salinger is famous for his style of writing, which combines acute observation with an _____ wit.

6. The pilots mentioned the _____ over the intercom, causing Enrique to cringe at the thought of being so high above the ground.

7. The tailor used his notepad to indicate the _____ that would be necessary for Jesse's wedding suit.

8. Although she is something of a celebrity, Kelly Osbourne is known as much for her _____ tongue as her music.

9. Nick had an _____ sense of smell: He could tell from a block away when Grandma Lachey was making his favorite strawberry-rhubarb pie.

10. We did not mean to _____ the ants, but when we accidentally stepped on their colony, they began to swarm around the opening.

11. Hilary's _____ decision to spend her weekend volunteering at the soup kitchen inspired her friends to similar charitable acts.

12. Ted Williams was renowned for his sharp eyes, for his visual _____ was key to his phenomenal ability as a batter.

13. The Mayans thrived in a mostly _____ society, although they hunted as well.

14. Because the English teacher was known for giving extra assignments for misbehavior or a poor attitude, her students tried hard not to _____ her.

15. Gwyneth's intellectual _____ and compassion led many to seek her advice.

16. When her metabolism began to slow down, Suzanne Somers had to _____ her diet to maintain her svelte physique.

17. Foreigners who enter the United States without legal permission are called illegal _____.

18. The weather _____ between hazy, sunny days and cold, rainy days.

19. Mountain climbing enthusiasts often carry an _____ with them so they can monitor their progress.

20. _____ accounts for a dwindling share of the U.S. economy.

Exercise B

Match the word with the letter of its definition.

1. ___ acerbity
2. ___ acrid
3. ___ acrimonious
4. ___ acumen
5. ___ acuity
6. ___ acute
7. ___ agility
8. ___ agitate
9. ___ agrarian
10. ___ agriculture
11. ___ alias
12. ___ alien
13. ___ alienate
14. ___ alter
15. ___ alteration
16. ___ alternate
17. ___ altimeter
18. ___ altitude
19. ___ altruistic
20. ___ exacerbate

a) to disturb or annoy
b) pertaining to the cultivation of the land
c) dire, severe
d) a change
e) a foreigner, a non-citizen
f) to change; to make different
g) bitterness, sourness
h) an assumed name or identity
i) bitter or nasty (in speech)
j) ability to move with grace and dexterity
k) an instrument used for measuring altitude
l) good judgment
m) to increase the severity of
n) to do by turns
o) sharp perception
p) unselfish
q) the practice of farming
r) stinging, harsh to the senses
s) to estrange
t) height, distance above sea/ ground level

Exercise C

Solve the crossword puzzle:

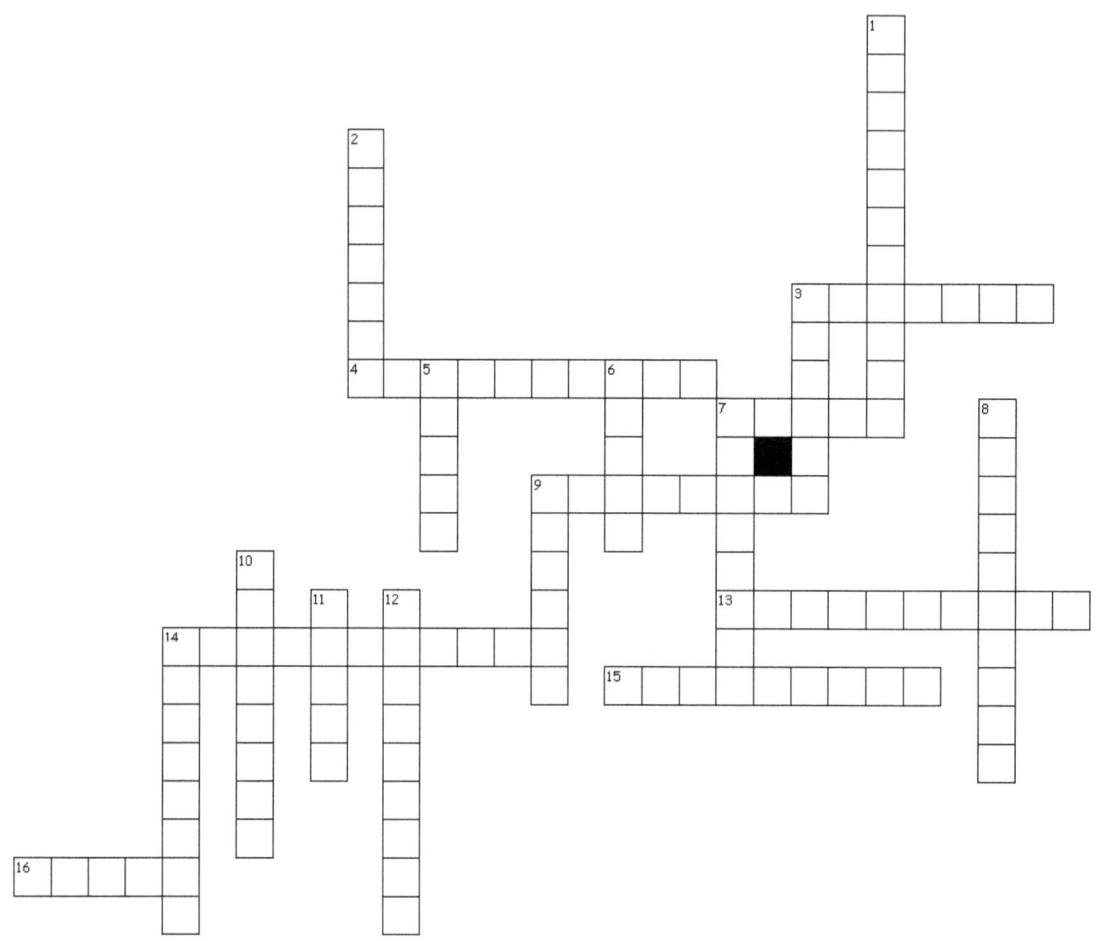

Across
3. ability to move with dexterity
4. to increase the severity of
7. an assumed name or identity
9. stinging, harsh to the senses
13. a change
14. the practice of farming
15. to do by turns
16. bitterness, sourness

Down
1. bitter or nasty (in speech)
2. to disturb or annoy
3. sharp perception
5. a foreigner, a non-citizen
6. to change; to make different
7. to estrange
8. unselfish
9. good judgment
10. the cultivation of land
11. dire, severe
12. used for measuring altitude
14. height, distance above sea level

Lesson II

amo/amor, amb/ambul, anim, annus/enn, aperio, apt

AMO, AMOR
love

AMB, AMBUL
walk

ANIM
mind; soul; will; spirit

ANNUS, ENN-
year

APERIO
open

APT
fit

---

amateur, amiable, amicable, amity, amorous, enamored,
ambulatory, perambulator, somnambulate,
animadversion, animate, animosity,
equanimity, unanimous, annual, annuity, perennial
aperture, aptitude, inept

Word Definitions

amateur **n.** a person who does an activity for love, not money; a person considered inept in a particular activity
adj. non-professional; inept, unskillful
"The tennis pro handily defeated the weekend warrior, a rank amateur."
amare to love

amiable **adj.** friendly and pleasant in manner
"I warmed to my new acquaintance quickly for he was an amiable fellow."
amicus friend

amicable **adj.** characterized by friendliness and absence of discord
"After an amicable divorce, the couple talked frequently and even spent holidays together for the children's sake."
amicus friend

amity **n.** friendly relations
"The once-bickering neighbors have reached a state of amity."
amicus friend

amorous	**adj.** showing or feeling loving or sexual desire "Casanova was renowned for his amorous exploits." *amor* love
enamored	**v.** to be filled with love or admiration for "After becoming enamored of another girl, Pete broke up with Ally." *amor* love
ambulatory	**adj.** walking or able to walk; movable, mobile "After the motorcycle accident, she was no longer ambulatory and had to use a wheelchair." *ambulare* to walk
perambulator	**n.** a baby carriage "A perambulator is ideal for new moms who love to walk and their babies, who often fall asleep in the fresh air." *perambulare* to walk about in, to tour < *ambulare* to walk
somnambulate	**v.** to sleep walk "Lady Macbeth somnambulated, wandering Dunsinane castle in her sleep." *somnambulism (n.), somnambulant (adj.)* *somnus* sleep + *ambulare* to walk
animadversion	**n.** strong criticism; a critical attitude or comment "The president's animadversion showed in his remarks to the Soviets." *animadvertere* to judge or punish: *animus* mind, spirit + *advertere* to turn to
animate	**v.** to give life or vigor to; to give the appearance of movement **adj.** alive or having life "After Matt drank coffee, his manner changed from dull to animated." *animation (n.)* *animare* to revive or rouse < *animus* spirit, mind, life
animosity	**n.** strong hostility "Dogs display animosity by baring their teeth and growling." *animus* spirit, mind
equanimity	**n.** calmness; composure; impartiality "A judge displays equanimity by acting in a calm, impartial manner." *aequi* equal, level + *animus* mind
unanimous	**adj.** fully in agreement; in universal or collective agreement "If everyone selects the same candidate, the vote is unanimous." *unanimity (n.)* *unanimus* acting in accord: *uni-* one + *animus* mind + *-ous*
annual	**adj.** occurring once every year; calculated over or covering a year; (of a plant) dying after one season or year (contrast with perennial) **n.** a book or magazine of a series published once a year; an annual plant "He descended into his annual bad temper every Christmas." *annus* year

LESSON II AMO/AMOR, AMB/AMBUL, ANIM, ANNUS/ENN, APERIO, APT

annuity **n.** a fixed sum of money paid to someone each year, typically for the rest of their lives; an investment that yields such an income
"A sizable <u>annuity</u> allowed him to draw a hefty annual income."
annus year

perennial **adj.** lasting for a long time; enduring or continually recurring; (of a plant) living for several or many years (contrast with annual)
n. a perennial plant
"The mayor was the <u>perennial</u> leader of the St. Patrick's Day parade."
perennis continual, perpetual: *per-* through + *annus* year

aperture **n.** an opening, hole, or gap
"The <u>aperture</u> of a camera is the lens opening where the light enters."
aperire to open

aptitude **n.** a natural ability or propensity
"A whiz with numbers, the girl showed a strong <u>aptitude</u> for mathematics."
aptus fitted < *apere* to fasten

inept **adj.** incompetent; awkward or clumsy
"The new kid proved <u>inept</u> as a catcher."
ineptitude (n.)
ineptus: in- not + *aptus* fitted < *apere* to fasten

Exercise A

Fill in the blanks in the sentences below with the correct form of a word in the scroll above.

1. Although Jennifer Lopez felt that she and Puff Daddy were on _____ terms, Puffy held a grudge after their sudden breakup.

2. Theodora's _____ income tripled in one year as a result of her increased sales.

3. Tom Brady's calmness and _____ under pressure help make him a great quarterback.

4. Bill Clinton's autobiography elicited _____ from some critics, but praise from others.

5. The first construction crew was so _____ that the entire addition had to be torn down and rebuilt by a more competent contractor.

6. The _____ favorites were sung with great enthusiasm every year.

7. Christopher Reeve, the star of the movie *Superman* who became paralyzed from the neck down, vowed to become fully _____ again.

8. When they shared the stage at the Video Music Awards, one could sense the _____ between the feuding divas, Lindsay and Hillary.

9. Sonya put up the hood on the _____ so her baby wouldn't get too much sun.

10. By adjusting the size of the camera _____ a photographer can control the amount of light that enters the lens when she releases the shutter.

11. Jessica was so in love that she spent all her free time writing _____ sonnets to her boyfriend.

12. After a year studying in London, Mike became so _____ of the city he began making plans to attend graduate school there.

13. The museum requested that the tour guides _____ their presentations to attract more visitors.

14. At the end of the gymnastics competition, the judges' decision was _____; the winner was evident.

15. Since my $10,000 _____ has a yield of 6 percent, I get a check for $600 each year.

16. Miriam was an _____ tennis player, but she yearned to become a professional some day.

17. Stephan's tendency to _____ concerned his parents as he sometimes sleepwalked down three flights of stairs.

18. Mozart had an innate _____ for music, and he displayed his dazzling talent at an extraordinarily young age.

19. His _____ disposition and charisma contributed to Tony Blair's success in establishing good relationships with other politicians.

20. Bill Clinton worked tirelessly to promote _____ in the Middle East, but despite his best efforts, peace remained elusive.

Exercise B

Match the word with the letter of its definition.

1. ___ amateur
2. ___ ambulatory
3. ___ amiable
4. ___ amicable
5. ___ amity
6. ___ amorous
7. ___ animadversion
8. ___ animate
9. ___ animosity
10. ___ annual
11. ___ annuity
12. ___ aperture
13. ___ aptitude
14. ___ enamored
15. ___ equanimity
16. ___ inept
17. ___ perambulator
18. ___ perennial
19. ___ somnambulate
20. ___ unanimous

a) having the capacity to walk
b) occurring every year
c) characterized by friendliness
d) incapable, unskilled
e) to give life to
f) peaceful relations
g) to walk in one's sleep
h) cordial, friendly
i) long-lasting
j) a non-professional person
k) a yearly payment of money
l) in love with or greatly admiring
m) an opening or hole
n) hatred
o) natural capacity or skill
p) indicating sexual desire or love
q) composure; calmness
r) in complete agreement
s) harsh criticism
t) baby carriage

Exercise C

Solve the crossword puzzle:

Across
1 A natural ability or propensity. 6 A fixed sum of money paid to someone each year, typically for the rest of their lives; an investment that yields such an income. 7 To sleep walk. 8 A person who does an activity for love, not money; a person considered inept in a particular activity Non-professional; inept, unskillful. 10 An opening, hole, or gap. 13 Showing or feeling loving or sexual desire. 14 A baby carriage. 15 Incompetent; awkward or clumsy. 17 Characterized by friendliness and absence of discord. 18 Fully in agreement; in universal or collective agreement. 19 Friendly relations. 20 To give life or vigor to; to give the appearance of movement; alive or having life.

Down
1 Strong hostility. 2 Dying after one season or year; a book or magazine of a series published once a year; an annual plant. 4 Strong criticism; a critical attitude or comment. 5 Walking or able to walk; movable, mobile 8 Friendly and pleasant in manner. 9 Lasting for a long time; enduring or continually recurring; living for several or many years. 11 Calmness; composure; impartiality. 12 To be filled with love or admiration for 16 Occurring once every year; calculated over or covering a year; dying after one season or year; a book or magazine of a series published once a year.

Lesson III

arm, art, aud/audit, aur, avuncular, basis, battuo, beatum

ARM **weapon**	*ART* **skill, craft**	*AUD, AUDIT* **hear**
AUR **gold**	*AVUNCULAR* **uncle**	
BASIS **base**	*BATTUO* **beat**	*BEATUM* **bless**

army, disarmament, artifact, artifice, artificial, artless, artisan, audial, audible, auditorium, audience, aureate, aureole, avuncular, debase, battery, battlement, abate, beatific, beatitude

Word Definitions

army **n.** an organized military force; a large number of similar people or things
"The highly unpopular politician faced an <u>army</u> of critics."
armare to arm

disarmament **n.** the reduction or withdrawal of military forces and weapons
"Nuclear <u>disarmament</u> is a pressing issue for democratic nations."
dis- not + *armare* to arm

artifact **n.** an object made by a human being
"Archaeological sites yielded <u>artifacts</u> crafted by ancient humans."
artificium art, craft, technologyl: *artis* craft, art + *factum* something made

artifice **n.** clever devices or expedients, especially to trick or deceive others
"The Trojan horse was Odysseus' <u>artifice</u> to get warriors inside the city."
ars, artis art + *facere* to make

artificial	**adj.** not natural; man-made; untruthful "Artificial flowers may deceive initially, but not on closer inspection." *ars, artis* art + *facere* to make
artisan	**n.** a skilled worker who makes things by hand; a craftsperson "Coopers, sail-makers and rope-makers were typical artisans of a whaling town." *artire* to instruct in the arts
artless	**adj.** without guile or pretense; clumsy; unsophisticated "Compared to the city mouse, the country mouse was artless." *ars, artis* art, craft + -less (without)
auditory	**adj.** relating to or perceived through the sense of hearing "His auditory nerves were damaged, so he had trouble hearing on the right side." *audire* to hear
audible	**adj.** able to be heard "The music was audible from across the lawn." *audire* to hear
audience	**n.** the assembled spectators or listeners at an event; the readership of a book, magazine, or newspaper; a formal interview with a person in authority "The Pope rarely grants an audience to ordinary churchgoers." *audire* to hear
auditorium	**n.** the part of a theater or hall in which an audience sits "The crowd milled about the auditorium while the musicians tuned up." *audire* to hear
aureate	**adj.** made of or having the color of gold; brilliant or splendid "Christian religious paintings feature angels with aureate halos." *aurum* gold
aureole	**n.** (in paintings) a radiant circle surrounding a person's head or body as a way of representing holiness; a corona around the sun or moon "In a solar eclipse, the aureole around the sun is pronounced." *aurum* gold
avuncular	**adj.** like an uncle in being kind and friendly towards a younger or less experienced person "Santa Claus is portrayed as a rosy-cheeked, avuncular figure." *avuncular* < *avunculus* maternal uncle
debase	**v.** to lower the quality, value, or character of "The scarlet letter was a token to debase Hester Prynne for adultery." *de-* down from + *base* foundation or pedestal
abate	**v.** (of something bad) to become less intense or widespread "After raging for three days, the fever abated." *a-* away from (expressing opposition) + *battuere* to beat or strike

LESSON III ARM, ART, AUD/AUDIT, AUR, AVUNCULAR, BASIS, BATTUO, BEATUM

battery   n. a container consisting of one or more cells in which chemical energy is converted into electricity and used as source of power; any large group of things; striking of one person by another; two or pieces of artillery
"Legally, an assault is a threat, while battery involves striking a person."
battuere to strike, pound or beat

battlement   n. a defensive wall with openings at regular intervals along the top, forming part of a fortification or castle
"Hamlet stood on Elsinore's battlement as the ghost of his father appeared."
battualia military exercises < *battuere* to beat

beatific   adj. feeling or expressing blissful happiness or exalted joy
"Botticelli painted rapturous saints with beatific smiles."
beatus blessed

beatitude   n. supreme blessedness or happiness; Jesus' proclamations of blessedness in the "Sermon on the Mount"
"One of the Beatitudes from the Gospel of Matthew is 'Blessed are the peacemakers, for they shall be called children of God.'"
beatitudo blessedness < *beatus* blessed

Exercise A

Fill in the blanks in the sentences below with the correct form of a word in the scroll above.

1. The _____ of the IRA and the unionists has made Ireland much safer.

2. Since the Industrial Revolution, handcrafted goods made by _____ have been largely replaced by manufactured items.

3. The child's _____ questions about her divorce disarmed Sheila, who normally found such inquiries painfully intrusive or offensive.

4. The radio requires either a _____ or an AC adapter for power.

5. The substitute teacher's pleas for order were barely _____ over the students' chatter.

6. The Buddhist monk radiated the _____ of one who has attained liberation from desire, pain and suffering.

7. The American _____ uses a combination of infantry, armored vehicles, and tactical weapons during combat.

8. The Dave Matthews Band performed before an enthusiastic _____ on Saturday.

9. The archers standing atop the _____ inflicted many casualties before their enemies even reached the tower gate.

10. Jessica's face lit up with a _____ smile when Nick proposed to her.

11. She used all her wiles and _____ to persuade the widowed millionaire to marry her.

12. The middle school raised enough money to build a new _____ so they could convene the growing student body.

13. Although meteorologists had predicted the blizzard would _____ in time to clear the roads before school Monday, the storm lingered and school was closed.

14. The viceroy refused to _____ or humiliate Lord Jeffrey for his defeat in battle, so the irate king had them both thrown in the dungeons for a fortnight.

15. Pottery and arrowheads were some of the most valuable _____ found at the prehistoric village.

16. Joan's uncle Herb, her guardian since her father had died, met with Joan before her wedding to dispense a bit of _____ advice.

17. The _____ dome of the capitol building in Boston is both a historic landmark and a source of pride for Bostonians.

18. In Renaissance paintings, saints and other religious figures are often seen with an _____ surrounding their heads.

19. The silk flowers in the arrangement, although _____ , are still attractive.

20. The pediatrician asked her nurse to screen Nick for possible _____ problems after he complained of a ringing sound in his ears.

LESSON III ARM, ART, AUD/AUDIT, AUR, AVUNCULAR, BASIS, BATTUO, BEATUM

Exercise B

Match the word with the letter of its definition.

1. ___ abate
2. ___ army
3. ___ artifact
4. ___ artifice
5. ___ artificial
6. ___ artisan
7. ___ artless
8. ___ audial
9. ___ audible
10. ___ audience
11. ___ auditorium
12. ___ aureate
13. ___ aureole
14. ___ avuncular
15. ___ battery
16. ___ battlement
17. ___ beatific
18. ___ beatitude
19. ___ disarmament
20. ___ debase

a) golden
b) something that produces electricity by chemical reaction
c) extreme happiness or blessedness
d) a halo of light that surrounds the head
e) the act of taking weapons away from a group or nation
f) a group of spectators
g) an organized group of trained soldiers
h) a defensive wall with regular openings at the top
i) showing joy or happiness
j) a deceitful stratagem
k) to decrease in intensity
l) a room used to accommodate an audience
m) to decrease the value of (something)
n) straightforward, lacking deceit
o) loud enough to be heard
p) acting like an uncle in being kind to a younger person
q) something made by a human
r) a craftsman or skilled worker
s) related to the sense of hearing
t) not natural; made as a copy

Exercise C

Solve the crossword puzzle.

Across
1. an organized group of soldiers
2. acting like an uncle in being king to a younger person
5. related to the sense of hearing
8. something made by a human
9. to decrease value of something
10. a group of spectators
11. a defensive wall with regular openings at the top
12. showing job or happiness
14. a room used to accommodate an audience
16. something that produces electricity by chemical reaction

Down
1. a craftsman or skilled worker
3. golden
4. to decrease in intensity
5. a deceitful stratagem
6. the act of taking weapons away from a group
7. loud enough to be heard
13. a halo of light that surrounds the
15. straightforward, lacking deceit
16. extreme happiness or blessedness

Lesson IV

belli, bibo, breve, cad/cas, calcitro, cand, canto

BELLI	*BIBO*	*BREVE*	*CAD, CAS*
war	drink	short	fall

CALCITRO	*CAND*	*CANTO*
kick	white, glow	sing

antebellum, bellicose, belligerent, rebellious, imbibe, abbreviate, abbreviation, brevity, cadence, cascade, casualty, decadent, deciduous, recalcitrant, candid, candidate, candor, incandescent, incantation, recant

Word Definitions

antebellum   **adj.** occurring or existing before a particular war (especially the U.S. Civil War)
"<u>Antebellum</u> Alabama had a larger slave than free white population."
ante- before + *bellum* war

bellicose   **adj.** warlike in manner or temperament; pugnacious
"<u>Bellicose</u> tribes of Turkic nomads allied with Genghis Khan, founder of the Mongolian Empire, to subjugate most of Asia and Eastern Europe."
bellicosity (n.)
bellum war

belligerent   **adj.** hostile and aggressive
n. a nation or person engaged in a war or conflict
"The two <u>belligerents</u> were finally brought to the peace table."
belligerence (n.)
belligerare to wage war < *bellum* war

rebellious   **adj.** showing a desire to rebel; often difficult to control, unmanageable
"A mutiny is a <u>rebellious</u> uprising to wrest command from the captain."
re- back, again (expressing repetition) + *bellum* war

imbibe	**v.** to drink (usually alcohol); to absorb (knowledge, ideas, etc.) "Shunning alcoholic drinks, Seventh Day Adventists do not <u>imbibe</u>." *imbibere*: *im-* in + *bibere* to drink
abbreviate	**v.** to shorten (a word, phrase, or text) "The skit was an <u>abbreviated</u> version of "Romeo and Juliet."" *abbreviare*: to shorten, cut off < *brevis* short
abbreviation	**n.** the act or product of shortening; a shortened form of a word "Etc. is an <u>abbreviation</u> for the Latin words 'et cetera.'" *abbreviare*: to shorten, cut off < *brevis* short
brevity	**n.** concise and exact use of words; the quality of being brief "The Gettysburg Address, which lasted only a few minutes, was a marvel of <u>brevity</u>." *brevis* brief, short
cadence	**n.** rhythm (of speech or verse); a fall in tone of voice "The lullaby's <u>cadence</u> relaxes her children and induces sleep." *cadere* to fall
cascade	**n.** a small waterfall, especially one in a series; a mass of something that falls, hangs, or occurs in copious quantities **v.** to pour downward rapidly and in large quantities "A small leak in the dike quickly grew into a torrential <u>cascade</u>." *cadere* to fall < *casus* fallen
casualty	**n.** a person killed or injured in a war or accident "It is said that in war the first <u>casualty</u> is the truth." *casus* fall, accident, emergency
decadent	**adj.** characterized by or reflecting a state of moral, cultural or physical decline; luxuriously self-indulgent "Young people celebrated a <u>decadent</u> lifestyle in the 'Roaring Twenties,' in reaction to the harsh privations, death and destruction of World War I." *decadence (n.)* *decadere* to fall down or off: *de-* from + *cadere* to fall
deciduous	**adj.** (of trees) shedding their leaves annually (opposite of evergreens) "Unlike <u>deciduous</u> varieties, this bamboo says green year round." *decidere* to fall down or off (variant of *decadere*)
recalcitrant	**adj.** obstinately uncooperative "The <u>recalcitrant</u> child stubbornly refused to obey the rules." *recalcitrance (n.)* *recalcitrare* to be disobedient, kick out with the heels < *calx, calcis* heel
candid	**adj.** truthful and straightforward; frank "Let's be <u>candid,</u> instead of beating around the bush." *candidus* transparent or white
candidate	**n.** a person who applies for a job or is nominated for election; a person or thing suitable for or likely to receive a particular fate, treatment, or position

LESSON IV BELLI, BIBO, BREVE, CAD/CAS, CALCITRO, CAND, CANTO

	"A scholar with strong social and leadership skills, he was a perfect <u>candidate</u> for university president." *candidatus* white-robed < *candidus* white, transparent
candor	**n.** the quality of being open and honest "Politicians are not known their <u>candor</u> in dealing with the media." *candor* honesty, purity, whiteness
incandescent	**adj.** emitting light as a result of being heated "The heating element in a toaster gives off an <u>incandescent</u> glow." *incandescence (n.)* *incandescere* to glow with light, to become hot
incantation	**n.** a series of words said as a magic spell or in a ritual "'Abracadabra' is a magician's standard <u>incantation</u>." *incantatory (adj.)* *incantare* to chant, bewitch < *cantare* to sing
recant	**v.** to renounce a former opinion or belief "Faced with torture, Joan of Arc <u>recanted</u> her claim of hearing voices." *recantation (n.)* *recantare* to revoke: *re-* (expressing reversal) + *cantare* to sing

Exercise A

Fill in the blanks in the sentences below with the correct form of a word in the scroll above.

1. Although a soldier may not be a _____ of war in the traditional sense, the psychological damage may be a life-long hardship.

2. The _____ for the United States of America is simply U.S.A.

3. Slavery was a prominent practice of the _____ South.

4. Health-minded people might consider a banana split the height of _____ desserts.

5. It is illegal for people under 21 to _____ alcoholic beverages in most states.

6. In *The Catcher in the Rye*, Holden Caulfield is portrayed as a depressed and _____ teenager who refuses to do what adults expect of him.

7. A _____ photo is one that is natural, not posed.

8. In autumn, _____ trees put on a show of color before losing their leaves.

9. Some politicians view filmmaker Michael Moore as _____ for his attacks on government policy and major corporations.

10. Even after the military failed to find weapons of mass destruction in Iraq, President Bush refused to _____ his claim that Saddam Hussein had stockpiled them.

11. Government agencies are fond of _____, but some acronyms are faintly ridiculous: for example, POTUS, short for "president of the United States."

12. The manager reprimanded the clerk for telling a customer she could buy the same toy for less at Wal-Mart, but the customer appreciated the clerk's _____.

13. Cornell University is famous for the _____ that abound in the parks surrounding the campus.

14. Jessica surprised the audience with the _____ of her song, which lasted only thirty seconds.

15. _____ light bulbs were first used at Biltmore in the 1890's, long before they were a standard feature in most American homes.

16. The two tribes, which had been _____ for centuries, were persuaded to join the governing coalition after much arm-twisting by U.N. negotiators.

17. Choosing a _____ for each party is the purpose of the primaries.

18. He likes to listen to the easy, pleasant _____ of The Eagles or Elton John.

19. As Gandalf spoke the _____, the wind swirled and the earth shook menacingly.

20. Known for his _____ behavior, Andrew was feared by his classmates, who did not want to become involved in a fight.

LESSON IV BELLI, BIBO, BREVE, CAD/CAS, CALCITRO, CAND, CANTO

Exercise B

Match the word with the letter of its definition.

1. ___ abbreviate
2. ___ abbreviation
3. ___ antebellum
4. ___ bellicose
5. ___ belligerent
6. ___ brevity
7. ___ cadence
8. ___ candid
9. ___ candidate
10. ___ candor
11. ___ cascade
12. ___ casualty
13. ___ decadent
14. ___ deciduous
15. ___ imbibe
16. ___ incandescent
17. ___ incantation
18. ___ rebellious
19. ___ recalcitrant
20. ___ recant

a) in a state of moral or cultural decline
b) to drink
c) before a war
d) the quality of being concise
e) rhythm
f) a shortened form of a word
g) obstinate, uncooperative
h) honest and frank
i) a person killed or injured
j) words of a spell or ritual
k) (of trees) losing their leaves each year
l) hostile and aggressive
m) warlike, pugnacious
n) glowing due to heat
o) to shorten, to decrease the length of
p) the quality of being frank
q) opposing authority
r) to take back a previous statement
s) a series of waterfalls
t) a person who is nominated for election

Exercise C

Solve the crossword puzzle:

Across

3. Showing a desire to rebel; difficult to control, unmanageable. 4. Occurring or existing before a particular war (especially the U.S. Civil War). 6. A modulation or inflection of the voice; rhythm. 7. Characterized by or reflecting a state of moral or cultural decline; luxuriously self-indulgent. 8. To drink (alcohol). 9. To shorten (a word, phrase, or text). 12. Emitting light as a result of being heated. 15. The quality of being open and honest. 16. Truthful and straightforward; frank. 17. To renounce a former opinion or belief. 18. Shedding its leaves annually (contrasted with evergreen). 19. A series of words said as a magic spell or ritual.

Down

1. A person who applies for a job or is nominated for election; a person or thing suitable for or likely to receive a particular fate, treatment, or position. 2. The act or product of shortening; a shortened form of a word. 5. Obstinately uncooperative. 6. A person killed or injured in a war or accident. 10. Concise and exact use of words. 11. Hostile and aggressive. 13. A small waterfall, especially one in a series; a mass of something that falls, hangs, or occurs in copious quantities. 14. Warlike in manner or temperament; pugnacious.

Lesson V
cap/cip, caput/capitis, carn, castigo, cerebrum, cern

CAP, CIP
to take

CAPUT, CAPITIS
head

CARN
flesh; meat

CASTIGO
to punish

CEREBRUM
brain

CERN
to discern

---

capture, deception, inception, participate, participation, recipient, decapitate, recapitulate, carnage, carnal, carnivorous, incarnate, castigate, chasten, cerebral, cerebration, ascertain, certitude, discreet, discretion

---

Word Definitions

capture
v. to take possession of or control; to seize by force, arrest
"The blurry photograph failed to <u>capture</u> her true beauty."
capere to seize, to take

deception
n. use of a ruse or trick; the action of deceiving
"Her <u>deception</u> was so ingenious that it took him months to uncover the lies she'd mixed with the truth."
deceptive (adj.)
decipere to deceive, to lead astray: *de-* from + *capere* to take

inception
n. the establishment or starting point of an institution or activity
"January 1, 2001 marked the <u>inception</u> of the twenty-first century."
incipere to begin, to undertake: *in-* in, upon + *capere* to take

participate
v. to share; to take part in
"Patriots dressed as Indians <u>participated</u> in the Boston Tea Party."
participatory (adj.)
participare to take part in: *pars, part-* part + *capere* to take

participation	**n.** the act of taking part in or sharing something "Your participation is welcome at our wedding. Please attend." *participatory (adj.)* *participare* to take part in: *pars, part-* part + *capere* to take
recipient	**n.** a receiver (of something) "Lance Armstrong was the ultimate recipient of the yellow jersey." *recipere* to take back, to accept: *re-* again + *capere* to take
decapitate	**v.** to cut off the head "The guillotine decapitated scores of aristocrats – as well as its inventor." *decapitation (n.)* *decapitare* to decapitate: *de-* away + *caput, capitis* head
recapitulate	**v.** to summarize by going over the main points again "The stages of a human embryo's development recapitulate earlier evolutionary forms." *recapitulation (n.)* *recapitulat* go through heading by heading: *re-* again + *capitulum* chapter, heading < *caput, capitis* head
carnage	**n.** the killing of a large number of people "Photographs of Dresden after the Allied bombings showed indiscriminate carnage." *carnalis* of the flesh < *caro, carnis* flesh
carnal	**adj.** relating to physical, especially sexual, needs and activities "'Carnal knowledge' is a formal term for sexual relations." *carnalis* of the flesh < *caro, carnis* flesh
carnivorous	**adj.** (of an animal) feeding on meat or other animal life "Unlike the brachiosaurus, whose diet consisted entirely of plants, the tyrannosaurus rex was carnivorous." *carnivorus* eating flesh: *caro, carn-* flesh + *vorare* to devour)
incarnate	**adj.** embodied in human form **v.** to embody or represent "Hitler was considered by many to be the devil incarnate." *incarnare* to make flesh: *in-* into + *caro, carnis* flesh
castigate	**v.** to reprimand or punish severely "Horrible machines of torture castigated medieval prisoners." *castigation (n.)* *castigare* to punish or correct < *castus* pure, chaste
chasten	**v.** to punish or subdue, reprove or restrain "The toddler happily dumped her soup on the floor, but was chastened by her mother's anger." *castigare* to punish or correct < *castus* pure, chaste

LESSON V CAP/CIP, CAPUT/CAPITIS, CARN, CASTIGO, CEREBRUM, CERN

cerebral adj. of the brain; intellectual rather than physical or emotional
"A scholar's work is <u>cerebral</u> rather than physical."
cerebrum brain

cerebration n. the working of the brain, thinking
"Group brainstorming is an act of communal <u>cerebration</u>."
cerebrate (v.)
cerebrum brain

ascertain v. to find out for certain; to determine
"From the map I <u>ascertained</u> the most direct route."
ascertainable (adj.), ascertainment (n.)
certus settled, sure, certain

certitude n. certainty; confidence; freedom from doubt
"He spoke with such <u>certitude</u> that it was clear nothing would change his mind."
certus settled, sure, certain

discreet adj. careful and prudent; set apart
"If Becky was to steal the cookies from the kitchen without being caught, she had to be <u>discreet</u>."
discernere to discern or distinguish: *dis-* apart + *cernere* to separate, discern

discretion n. the quality of being discreet; tactfulness; diplomacy; the freedom to decide on a course of action
"The length of the prison sentence was left to the judge's <u>discretion</u>."
discernere to discern or distinguish: *dis-* apart + *cernere* to separate, discern

Exercise A

Fill in the blanks in the sentences below with the correct form of a word in the scroll above.

1. Islamic extremists have been known to _____ their hostages.

2. The pirate ship used cunning and _____ to lure the British battleship into their ambush.

3. The _____ of the modern Olympics was a series of athletic contests organized in Athens, Greece, in 1896.

4. After two weeks of testimony, the judge asked the prosecutor and defense attorney to _____ their main points for the jury.

5. The Greeks were able to _____ Troy by withdrawing most of their forces, but leaving an apparent gift outside the city gates: a huge wooden horse containing soldiers, who opened the city gates after the Trojans dragged the horse inside.

6. Her father _____ Susan for going to the movies the night before her math test, instead of studying.

7. Although all dogs are _____ by nature, real meat is still a treat for most pets.

8. Drinking and dancing were viewed as _____ sins by the Puritans.

9. Although the Yankees expected a locker-room tirade after they lost the World Series, they wished owned George Steinbrenner would be more _____ in his comments to the media.

10. In high school, Britney Spears _____ in varsity basketball and other sports.

11. Hoping to enrage their fellow colonists and urge them to action, the separatists portrayed the Boston massacre as _____ by the British troops.

12. In the New Testament, Jesus is depicted as God _____, come to earth to share in the sufferings of humankind, teach us, and redeem our sins.

13. *The Return of the King* was the _____ of an astonishing eleven Academy Awards, winning every category in which it was nominated.

14. Although the widow appeared shocked at the news of her husband's death, the detective was able to _____ that she had no alibi.

15. The world's tallest man grew to a height of 8'4" because of slight _____ damage during brain surgery.

16. _____ is a medical term for "thinking" or the processes of the brain.

17. The more the teacher tried to _____ his students, the worse they behaved.

18. Celebrities value friends who understand the need for _____ and don't gossip about their private lives.

19. One can never have complete _____ about the future of the stock market, so it's important to invest in a balanced portfolio.

20. Their _____ in past demonstrations made them good targets for surveillance.

LESSON V CAP/CIP, CAPUT/CAPITIS, CARN, CASTIGO, CEREBRUM, CERN

Exercise B

Match the word with the letter of its definition.

1. ___ ascertain
2. ___ capture
3. ___ carnage
4. ___ carnal
5. ___ carnivorous
6. ___ castigate
7. ___ cerebral
8. ___ cerebration
9. ___ certitude
10. ___ chasten
11. ___ decapitate
12. ___ deception
13. ___ discreet
14. ___ discretion
15. ___ incarnate
16. ___ inception
17. ___ participate
18. ___ participation
19. ___ recapitulate
20. ___ recipient

a) a person who receives something
b) to repeat in summarized form
c) the use of illusion or trickery
d) eating mostly meat
e) a feeling of absolute certainty
f) having to do with the brain
g) massive slaughter or killing
h) to take by force, seize
i) to cut the head off
j) the quality of being discreet
k) careful and prudent
l) pertaining to the desires of the body
m) embodied in flesh
n) a beginning, a commencement
o) to have a demoralizing effect on
p) to reprimand severely
q) to take part in an activity
r) the act of thinking
s) the act of taking part or sharing in something
t) to discover, to gain knowledge of

Exercise C

Solve the crossword puzzle:

Across

3. The quality of being discreet; the freedom to decide on a course of action. 5. Careful and prudent. 8. Of the brain; intellectual rather than physical or emotional. 9. Embodied in human form. 10. A receiver of something. 12. To find out for certain. 13. To partake of. 14. (of an animal) Feeding on flesh. 15. The killing of a large number of people. 16. To reprimand severely. 17. Relating to physical, especially sexual, needs and activities.

Down

1. The action of deceiving. 2. A feeling of absolute certainty. 4. The working of the brain, thinking. 5. To cut off the head. 6. The establishment or starting point of an institution or activity. 7. The act of taking part or sharing something. 10. To summarize by restating the main points. 11. To have a restraining or demoralizing effect on. 15. To take possession of or control by force.

Lesson VI
ced, celer, censeo

CED
to yield, go

CELER
swift

CENSEO
to estimate

accede, access, accession, accessory, cede, concede, concession, precede, proceed, procession, recede, recession, celerity, accelerate, decelerate, censor, censorious, censure, census

Word Definitions

accede
v. to assent or agree to; to yield; to assume an office
"Elizabeth <u>acceded</u> to the throne upon the death of her half-sister, Mary."
accedere to approach, add to: *ad-* to (expressing intensity) + *cedere* to give way, yield

access
n. the means or opportunity to approach or enter a place; to retrieve information stored in a computer
v. to approach or enter (a place)
"Only men and male animals get <u>access</u> to Mt. Athos monastery."
accedere to approach, add to: *ad-* toward + *cedere* to give way, yield

accession
n. the attainment of a position or office; an addition; an agreemen
v. to formally accept a treaty, or a contribution
"The 'Mona Lisa' was an early <u>accession</u> to the Louvre."
accedere to approach, add to: *ad-* to + *cedere* to give way, yield

accessory
n. a thing which can be added to something else, making it more useful, versatile, or attractive
adj. subsidiary or supplementary
"Chris thought the outfit very plain, but the sales clerk showed her how a few <u>accessories</u> – a jazzy handbag and belt – could dress it up."
accedere approach, add to: *ad-* to + *cedere* to give way, yield

cede	**v.** to give up (power or territory) "Texas was <u>ceded</u> to the US by Mexico." *cedere* to yield
concede	**v.** to admit the truth of something; to admit defeat; to grant a right "After intense interrogation, the suspect <u>conceded</u> his guilt." *concedere*: to relinquish, to pardon < *cedere* to yield
concession	**n.** a thing that is conceded; a preferential position or price "Emily holds the airport <u>concession</u> for shoe shine stands." *concedere*: to relinquish; to pardon < *cedere* to yield
precede	**v.** to go before in time, order, or position "Twenty-five letters of the English alphabet <u>precede</u> 'Z'." *praecedere*: to precede; to surpass: *prae-* before + *cedere* to go
proceed	**v.** to begin a course of action; to move forward **n.** (plural) gain or profit "After securing funding, she told Barbara to <u>proceed</u> with the project." *procedere* to proceed, advance: *pro-* forward + *cedere* to go
procession	**n.** a number of people or vehicles moving forward in an orderly fashion, especially as part of a ceremony or formal proceeding "A <u>procession</u> of witnesses was called in the trial of Leopold and Loeb." *procedere* to proceed, advance: *pro-* forward + *cedere* to go
recede	**v.** to move back or further away; to gradually diminish "As men age, the hairline tends to <u>recede</u> and expose bald scalp." *recedere* to go back, withdraw: *re-* back + *cedere* to go
recession	**n.** a period of economic decline during which trade and industrial activity are reduced "A <u>recession</u> followed the dot.com bust." *recedere* to go back, withdraw: *re-* back + *cedere* to go
celerity	**n.** swiftness of movement "She covered the distance with grace and <u>celerity</u>." *celer* swift
accelerate	**v.** to speed up "The spread of a fire can be <u>accelerated</u> with gasoline." *acceleration (n.)* *accelerare* to hasten: *ad-* toward + *celer* swift
decelerate	**v.** to slow down "Brakes <u>decelerate</u> a moving vehicle and bring it to a stop." *deceleration (n.)* *de-* away + *celer* swift
censor	**n.** an official who examines material before publication in order to suppress parts deemed offensive or a threat to security **v.** to examine (a book, film, etc.) and suppress portions of it "Vulgar language on daytime TV is typically <u>censored</u> with a bleeping

LESSON VI CED, CELER, CENSEO

noise."
censere to assess or judge

censorious **adj.** severely critical
"The judge directed his censorious remarks to the unprepared lawyer."
censor magistrate or critic + -ious

censure **v.** to express severe disapproval of; to reprimand formally
n. a formal reprimand
"His colleagues censured the senator for misleading investigators."
censere to assess or judge

census **n.** an official count or survey of a population
"The U.S. Constitution mandates a census every decade to ensure that each congressional district represents about the same number of people."
censere to assess

Exercise A

Fill in the blanks in the sentences below with the correct form of a word in the scroll above.

1. Only highly trusted employees have _____ to casino vaults.

2. Once all the members of the band had congregated, they _____ to the beginning of the parade route.

3. The town conducted an annual _____ to determine whether its population was growing or shrinking.

4. During hurricanes, a calm period often _____ the most destructive part of the storm.

5. Although computers have become less expensive, the prices of optional _____ have remained the same or gone up.

6. Jan _____ to Dan's request that they go to Little Italy for his birthday dinner, even though tomato sauce gave her heartburn.

7. The professor was the most _____ at the elite school, always finding fault with students' grammar or etiquette.

8. The train was forced to _____ rapidly when the engineer saw that the bridge ahead had collapsed.

9. When Germany lost World War II, it had to _____ some of its most fertile land to neighboring countries.

10. Queen Victoria's _____ to the throne occurred when she was quite a young woman.

11. Tim's decision to quit the wrestling team was met with severe _____ by his parents, who thought the sport provided him with much-needed discipline.

12. Baldness does not preclude stardom: Yule Brynner, Bruce Willis, Nicholas Cage, and Robert De Niro all enjoyed great success as their hairlines _____.

13. The environmental bill could not pass until each political party made _____.

14. The gala _____ began at the school and continued through downtown to City Hall.

15. Al Gore refused to _____ defeat to George W. Bush until the Supreme Court upheld Bush's victory in Florida.

16. In our country, it is unacceptable to _____ individual expression of political views.

17. To get out of the way quickly and prevent an accident, the sports car had to _____.

18. Olympic skier Picabo Street's _____ on the slopes is awe inspiring.

19. When economic growth slows for two quarters in a row, the trend is called a _____.

Exercise B

Match the word with the letter of its definition.

1. ___ accede
2. ___ accelerate
3. ___ access
4. ___ accession
5. ___ accessory
6. ___ cede
7. ___ celerity
8. ___ censor
9. ___ censorious
10. ___ censure
11. ___ concede
12. ___ concession
13. ___ census
14. ___ decelerate
15. ___ precede
16. ___ proceed
17. ___ procession
18. ___ recede
19. ___ recession

a) a supplementary, nonessential item
b) to examine and suppress parts of a book
c) an admission or acknowledgment
d) to go before
e) to begin a course of action
f) a period of economic decline
g) a way to enter or use (something)
h) people or vehicles moving forward in an orderly fashion
i) to move back or further away
j) to give up possession of
k) to slow down
l) swiftness, quickness
m) to speed up
n) to give way to the wishes of another
o) strict, highly critical
p) the attainment of a position of rank
q) to admit or acknowledge
r) to reprimand formally
s) an official count of a population

Exercise C

Solve the crossword puzzle:

Across
1 An official count or survey of a population 4 To assent or agree to; to yield; to assume an office 7 Swiftness of movement 8 To go before in time, order, or position 10 The means or opportunity to approach or enter a place; to retrieve information stored in a computerv. to approach or enter (a place) 11 To begin a course of action; to move forward; gain or profit 14 Severely critical 15 To speed up 16 The attainment of a position or office; an addition; an agreement; to formally accept a treaty, or a contribution 17 A thing that is conceded; a preferential position or price 18 To admit the truth of something; to admit defeat; to grant a right

Down
1 To give up (power or territory) 2 To move back or further away; to gradually diminish 3 An official who examines material before publication in order to suppress parts deemed offensive or a threat to security; to examine (a book, film, etc.) and suppress portions of it 5 To express severe disapproval of; to reprimand formally; a formal reprimand 6 A period of economic decline during which trade and industrial activity are reduced 9 A thing which can be added to something else, making it more useful, versatile, or attractive; subsidiary or supplementary 12 People or vehicles going forward in an orderly way, especially as part of a ceremony or formal proceeding 13 Slow down

Lesson VII
cent, cid/cis, cit/cital, civi

CENT	CID, CIS	CIT, CITAL	CIVI
one hundred	to cut, kill	to call, start	citizen

bicentennial, centenary, centennial, centigrade, centipede, century, concise, herbicide, homicide, incise, incision, precise, suicide, incite, excite, recitation, recite, civil, civilian, civilization

Word Definitions

bicentennial n. the two-hundredth anniversary
"The year 2003 marked the bicentennial of the Louisiana Purchase."
bi- two + *centum* one hundred

centenary n. the hundredth anniversary; a period of 100 years
adj. occurring every hundred years
"On the centenary of my grandmother's birth, we threw a party for her."
centum one hundred

centennial n. a centary; the completion of a 100-year period
adj. marking the completion of 100 years
"The centennial celebration of Custer's last stand occurred in 1876."
centum one hundred

centigrade adj. a temperature scale that denotes the freezing point of water as 0 degrees
"The Centigrade scale is far more rational than the Fahrenheit scale."
centum one hundred + *gradus* step

centipede n. an arthropod with a flattened, elongated body composed of many segments, most of which bear a pair of legs
"She overturned the log, revealing dozens of centipedes."
centipedis hundred-footed: *centum* one hundred + *pes, pedis* foot

century	**n.** a period of one hundred years "The century plant blooms roughly every hundred years." *centum* one hundred
concise	**adj.** giving information clearly and in a few words "A concise history of the flea: 'Adam had 'em.'" *concision (n.)* *concidere* to cut down; to collapse
herbicide	**n.** a toxic substance used to destroy unwanted plants "Boiling water will eliminate weeds as well as chemical herbicides." *herbicidal (adj.)* *herba* herb + *caedere* to cut down or kill
homicide	**n.** the killing of another human being "In the Bible, Cain committed the first homicide by killing Abel." *homicidal (adj.)* *homicidium*: to kill a person: *homo, homin-* man + *caedere* to kill
incise	**v.** to make a cut or cuts in (a surface) "The lovers incised a heart with their initials into the tree trunk." *incidere* to cut into
incision	**n.** a surgical cut "The surgeon was nervous about making the incision, for she knew if her cut was even a centimeter off, she risked the patient's life." *incidere* to cut into
precise	**adj.** marked by exactness and accuracy of expression or detail "Diamond cutting is a precise art." *precision (n.)* *praecidere* to cut short: *prae-* before, in front of + *incidere* to cut
suicide	**n.** to kill oneself intentionally "The kamikaze were Japanese pilots who committed suicide by flying planes loaded with explosives into Allied warships and other targets." *suicidal (adj.)* *sui* of oneself + *caedere* to kill
incite	**v.** to encourage or stir up "Revere, Prescott, and Dawes incited the colonists to take up arms." *incitation (n.)* *incitare*: *in-* toward + *citare* to rouse, to call
excite	**v.** to cause to feel enthusiastic and eager; to awaken or arouse "The boy was so excited about Christmas, he couldn't get to sleep." *excitare* to excite: *ex-* out + *citare* to rouse, to call
recitation	**n.** the act of reciting memorized materials in a public performance "In some operas, singing is interspersed with recitation." *recitare* to read out: *re-* (expressing intensive force) + *citare* to cite

recite	**v.** to repeat aloud; to say from memory "POWs are told to recite only their name, rank, and serial number." *recitare* to read out: *re-* (expressing intensive force) + *citare* to cite
civil	**adj.** relating to ordinary citizens, as distinct from military, religious, or criminal matters; courteous and polite "Civil courts decide lawsuits between businesses or individuals; criminal courts decide crimes." *civis* citizen
civilian	**n.** a person not in the armed services or the police force **adj.** relating to citizens "When on leave at home, soldiers are required to wear civilian clothes, or 'civvies,' instead of their uniforms." *civis* citizen
civilization	**n.** an advanced stage or system of human social development; a particular culture or society "Ancient Greek civilization is credited with advancing the arts, sciences, philosophy, and mathematics." *civis* citizen

Exercise A

Fill in the blanks in the sentences below with the correct form of a word in the scroll above.

1. A 1997 book celebrates the _____ of Queen Victoria's Silver Jubilee in 1897, which included ceremonies intended to demonstrate the British Empire's power.

2. The doctors made an _____ in Daniel's abdomen to extract the bullet from his spleen.

3. The fifth _____ A.D. saw the fall of the Roman Empire, one of the greatest civilizations on Earth.

4. Merely the thought of the upcoming basketball season was enough to _____ Jack Nicholson, a die-hard Lakers' fan.

5. Sally fell into a deep depression after her husband died, and her friends became concerned that she was contemplating _____.

6. One of the beasts in "Monsters, Inc." was a grotesque _____ whose numerous legs and spindly body left children quivering with fear.

7. The attacks of Sept. 11 caused more _____ casualties than any previous terrorist attack against the United States.

8. The _____ essay was short, but well-organized.

9. Steve had memorized his poem, but he was still anxious that his voice would crack during the _____.

10. Ford Motor Co. celebrated its _____ in 2003 by manufacturing a special edition F-150 truck.

11. Chinese _____ was thriving as European nations, ravaged by the bubonic plague, entered the Dark Ages.

12. The Yankee fan's verbal abuse of the Red Sox player _____ a riot in the bleachers.

13. Bob used an _____ to kill the chickweed in his garden before planting his begonias.

14. America is one of a few countries that still measures temperature according to the Fahrenheit scale instead of _____.

15. The best detectives on the police force are recommended to serve in the _____ unit.

16. The U.S. Supreme Court has the responsibility of protecting the _____ rights of all citizens, including criminals.

17. In 1976, America celebrated the _____ of its independence.

18. Each child was asked to _____ his or her favorite classic story in front of the class.

19. The _____ location of the hidden treasure had eluded the islanders for many years.

20. One of the most artistic Native American artifacts is a type of stone tool _____ with intricate decorations.

Exercise B

Match the word with the letter of its definition.

1. ___ bicentennial
2. ___ centenary
3. ___ centennial
4. ___ centigrade
5. ___ centipede
6. ___ century
7. ___ civil
8. ___ civilian
9. ___ civilization
10. ___ concise
11. ___ excite
12. ___ herbicide
13. ___ homicide
14. ___ incise
15. ___ incision
16. ___ incite
17. ___ precise
18. ___ recitation
19. ___ recite
20. ___ suicide

a) to make a cut or cuts
b) happening every two hundred years
c) expressed in few words
d) a chemical substance which kills plants
e) the hundredth anniversary
f) a 100-year period
g) the act of speaking from memory
h) a crawling insect with many feet
i) to repeat aloud
j) a surgical cut
k) the act of killing
l) clearly expressed or definite
m) relating to ordinary citizens
n) happening every one hundred years
o) a non-military resident of a country
p) to provoke
q) denoting a scale of temperature
r) to awaken or arouse
s) the act of killing oneself
t) a nation where people have reached a high level of development

Exercise C

Solve the crossword puzzle.

Across
4. A toxic substance used to destroy unwanted plants. 5. The hundredth anniversary. 6. A person not in the armed services or the police force. 7. Relating to a hundredth anniversary. 11. A surgical cut made in skin or flesh. 13. The killing of another human being . 14. To cause to feel very enthusiastic and eager. 16. To make a cut or cuts in (a surface). 18. To repeat aloud. 19. The act of reciting memorized materials in a public performance.

Down
1. A temperature scale that uses 0 degrees to denote the freezing temperature of water. 2. Giving information clearly and in a few words. 3. Relating to ordinary citizens, as distinct from military, religious or criminal matters; courteous and polite. 6. An arthropod with a flattened, elongated body composed of many segments, most of which bear a pair of legs. 8. Relating to a two-hundredth anniversary. 9. To encourage or stir up. 10. The action of killing oneself intentionally. 12. An advanced stage or system of human social development. 15. A period of one hundred years. 17. Marked by exactness and accuracy of expression or detail.

Lesson VIII
clam, clar, claud, clavis

CLAM	CLAR	CLAUD	CLAVIS
to cry out	to clean	to close, shut	key

acclaim, acclamation, clamor, clamorous, declaim, declamation clarify, clarion, clarity, claustrophobia, cloister, closure, enclose, enclosure, occlude, recluse, reclusion, clavicle, clavier, enclave

Word Definitions

acclaim
   v. to praise enthusiastically and publicly
   n. widespread public praise
   "Lindberg was <u>acclaimed</u> for his solo Atlantic flight."
   acclamare to shout approval: *ad-* to + *clamare* to shout out or proclaim

acclamation
   n. a shout or salute of enthusiastic approval; vote by unanimous voice
   "The measure recognizing the men as heroes passed by <u>acclamation</u>."
   acclamare to shout approval: *ad-* to + *clamare* to shout out or proclaim

clamor
   n. a loud confused noise, especially of shouting
   v. to shout or demand loudly
   "A <u>clamor</u> erupted in the stands after the last-minute touchdown."
   clamare to shout out or proclaim

clamorous
   adj. making or marked by loud outcry or sustained din
   "The trading floor of the stock market was <u>clamorous</u>."
   clamare to shout out or proclaim

declaim
   v. to deliver words in a rhetorical or impassioned way
   "At his inaugural, the president <u>declaimed</u> in classical style."
   declamare to make speeches; to bluster: *de-* (expressing intensity) + *clamare* to proclaim

declamation
   n. the action or art of recitation; oratory
   "The orator Cicero is the best-known exemplar of <u>declamation</u>."

	declamare to make speeches; to bluster: *de-* (expressing intensity) + *clamare* to proclaim
clarify	**v.** to make more comprehensible; to separate out impurities "Butter is clarified by heating and skimming off the milk solids." *clarification (n.)* *clarus* clear
clarion	**adj.** loud and clear **n.** a medieval trumpet with a clear, high tone "The bugle sounded the clarion call for the soldiers to charge." *clarus* clear
clarity	**n.** the state or quality of being clear, distinct, and easily perceived or understood; transparency "Even at age 90, the scholar showed great clarity of mind." *clarus* clear
claustrophobia	**n.** extreme or irrational fear of confined places "Those with claustrophobia shun elevators, caves, and closets." *claustrophobic (adj.)* *claustrum* lock, bolt + *-phobia* (from the Greek for fear)
cloister	**n.** a covered, and typically colonnaded, passage round an open court in a convent, monastery, college, or cathedral **v.** to seclude or shut up in a convent or monastery "A medieval woman's choice was marriage or the cloister." *claudere* or *cludere* to shut or close
closure	**n.** the act or process of closing; a feeling that an experience has been resolved "The divorce decree signaled closure for their marriage, but not their relationship as parents." *claudere* or *cludere* to shut or close
enclose	**v.** to surround or close off on all sides; to place an object inside a container or envelope "The medieval castle was enclosed by a moat to deter attacks." *includere* or *inclaudere* to shut in: *in-* in + *claudere* to close
enclosure	**n.** an area that is sealed off by a barrier; a document or object placed in an envelope together with a letter "A barbed wire enclosure surrounded the prison camp." *includere* or *inclaudere* to shut in: *in-* in + *claudere* to close
occlude	**v.** to block off, close up, or obstruct "You need a plunger or plumbing snake to open an occluded drain." *occludere* to close up: *ob-* against + *cludere* to close
recluse	**n.** a person who avoids others and lives a solitary life; a hermit "A hermit disdains company and lives as a recluse."

LESSON VIII CLAM, CLAR, CLAUD, CLAVIS

	reclusive (adj.) *recludere* to enclose: *re-* again + *cludere* to shut
reclusion	**n.** the condition of being a recluse "She went into reclusion every winter to meditate, and practice yoga." *recludere* to enclose: *re-* again + *cludere* to shut
clavicle	**n.** a medical term for the collarbone "The wishbone of a turkey is its clavicle." *clavis* key or lever
clavier	**n.** The keyboard of instruments including the piano, organ, and harpsichord; the arrangement of levers used to play the carillon "Although the claviers of the piano and organ appear similar, the mechanism underlying them is completely different." *clavis* key or lever
enclave	**n.** a territory surrounded by a larger one whose inhabitants are culturally or ethnically distinct; a group or area that is distinct from those surrounding it (a male enclave) "Monte Carlo is an exclusive enclave for the rich and famous." *in-* in, among + *clavis* key

Exercise A

Fill in the blanks in the sentences below with the correct form of a word in the scroll above.

1. Directors occasionally choose to _____ what is going on in a movie by making use of a narrator or voice-over.

2. As the Nobel Prize winner finished speaking, the students leaped up and shouted their _____.

3. After adjusting the microscope carefully, Peter could see the parasite with great _____.

4. His arteries were almost completely _____ by plaque, so the surgeon performed an emergency triple bypass.

5. As Patterson infiltrated the private hunting _____, he confirmed his suspicion that several shady deals had been orchestrated by the members.

6. "Fahrenheit 9/11" was met with the longest and most _____ ovation ever given at the Cannes Film Festival.

7. In "Hatchet", by Gary Paulson, the narrator lives in _____ from society, not by choice but by necessity, after his airplane crash-lands in the wilderness.

8. Pedro was relieved to learn that he and his family would be able to tour the abbey during the rain, sheltered by the _____ connecting the wings.

9. When Martin Luther King Jr. _____ his dream of equality, his extraordinary oratory moved ordinary people to join the struggle for racial equality.

10. Although Betsey expected to find solitude in the wilderness, she occasionally came upon a _____ who survived by hunting and gathering wild plants.

11. The _____ of a carillon consists of large levers arranged like the keys of a piano. When they are struck, the levers pull wires attached to clappers, ringing the bells.

12. As he crawled through the tiny tunnels beneath the jungle floor, the private was overcome with _____ when he realized he could be buried alive.

13. The construction crew missed the deadline to _____ the Olympic swimming pool with a fence.

14. The president's _____ honored the victims of the terrorist attacks.

15. Her Carnegie Hall premier was greeted with critical _____ .

16. The report condemned the school administration and sounded a _____ call for change.

17. Trying to block a goal, he landed on his shoulder and broke his _____.

18. After years of group therapy, she found a sense of _____ about her son's death.

19. During the winter, the sheep exercised in an _____ near the barn.

20. The _____ of the crowd grew ugly after the theater manager said the band was two hours behind schedule.

Exercise B

Match the word with the letter of its definition.

1. ___ acclaim
2. ___ acclamation
3. ___ clamor
4. ___ clamorous
5. ___ clarify
6. ___ clarion
7. ___ clarity
8. ___ claustrophobia
9. ___ clavicle
10. ___ clavier
11. ___ cloister
12. ___ closure
13. ___ declaim
14. ___ declamation
15. ___ enclave
16. ___ enclose
17. ___ enclosure
18. ___ occlude
19. ___ recluse
20. ___ reclusion

a) a formal speech; oratory
b) the keyboard of a musical instrument
c) to stop, close up, or obstruct
d) ease of perception, clearness
e) a covered walkway
f) a person who separates from society
g) to make more comprehensible
h) loud; of a sustained din
i) a speech marked by strong feeling
j) a shout of approval
k) a state of separation from society
l) to surround on all sides
m) a fear of enclosed places
n) to praise enthusiastically and publicly
o) a feeling that an experience has been resolved
p) a loud confused noise
q) a medical term for collarbone
r) an area sealed off by a barrier
s) loud and clear
t) a bounded area enclosed within a larger unit

Exercise C

Solve the crossword puzzle.

Across

3. A medical term for collarbone. 7. To make more comprehensible; to separate out the impurities. 9. A smaller territory surrounded by a larger one whose inhabitants are culturally or ethnically distinct; a group or area that is different in character from those surrounding it (a male enclave). 11. The act or process of closing; a feeling that an experience has been resolved. 12. To praise enthusiastically and publicly. 13. A covered, and typically colonnaded, passage round an open court in a convent, monastery, college, or cathedral. 14. To stop, close up, or obstruct. 16. A person who avoids others and lives a solitary life. 18. A shout or salute of enthusiastic approval. 19. The condition of being a recluse; solitary confinement.

Down

1. The state or quality of being clear, distinct, and easily perceived or understood; transparency. 2. To deliver words in a rhetorical or impassioned way. 4. Extreme or irrational fear of confined places. 5. Making or marked by a loud outcry or sustained din. 6. The action or art of declaiming. 8. An instrumental keyboard. 9. An area that is sealed off by a barrier; a document or object placed in an envelope together with a letter. 10. To surround or close off on all sides; to place an object inside a container or envelope. 15. Loud and clear. 17. A loud confused noise, especially of shouting.

Test 1

Choose the correct meaning for the underlined vocabulary word in each sentence.

1. "'You are ignorant,' Miss Bordereau remarked; not with <u>acerbity</u> but with a strange, soft coldness."

   The Aspern Papers by Henry James

   (a) bitterness (b) unpleasantness (c) trouble (d) haste (e) vigor

2. "With all respect for your natural <u>acumen</u>, I do not think that you are quite a match for the worthy doctor."

   The Return of Sherlock Holmes by Sir Arthur Conan Doyle

   (a) talent (b) agility (c) insight (d) calmness (e) rudeness

3. "There was an <u>acute</u> interest in all their faces during this exchange of view points."

   The Red Badge of Courage by Stephen Crane

   (a) fantastic (b) judgmental (c) cautious (d) kindly (e) intense

4. "An <u>altruistic</u> act is an act performed for the welfare of others."

   The Sea Wolf by Jack London

   (a) justified (b) alternative (c) unfamiliar (d) selfless (e) foreign

5. "He said nothing, however, and his conduct greatly astonished me; yet I thought it prudent not to <u>exacerbate</u> the growing moodiness of his temper by any comment."

   The Gold Bug by Edgar Allan Poe

   (a) critique (b) aggravate (c) perceive (d) drive (e) modulate

6. "But one fact was indubitable – she was in <u>amicable</u> relations with the highest dignitaries of all the churches and sects."

   Anna Karenina by Leo Tolstoy

55

(a) unlikely   (b) difficult   (c) friendly   (d) foreign   (e) strained

7. "She handled her brushes with a certain ease and freedom which came, not from long and close acquaintance with them, but from a natural <u>aptitude</u>."

The Awakening and Selected Short Stories by Kate Chopin

(a) knowledge   (b) intelligence   (c) resource   (d) ability   (e) guide

8. "But roses only bloom in summer; whereas the fine carnation of their cheeks is <u>perennial</u> as sunlight in the seventh heavens."

Moby Dick by Herman Melville

(a) bright   (b) colorful   (c) enduring   (d) loving   (e) inconsistent

9. "He had long experienced, that when the storm grew very high, arguments were but wind, which served rather to increase, than to <u>abate</u> it."

The History of Tom Jones by Henry Fielding

(a) decrease   (b) rate   (c) advance   (d) change   (e) test

10. "It was one of those rare afternoons when all the thickness and shadow of London are changed to a kind of shining, pulsing, special atmosphere; when the smoky vapors become fluttering golden clouds, nacreous veils of pink and amber; when all that bleakness of gray stone and dullness of dirty brick trembles in <u>aureate</u> light, and all the roofs and spires, and one great dome, are floated in golden haze."

Alexander's Bridge by Willa Cather

(a) radiant   (b) circular   (c) golden   (d) intense   (e) coming from the moon

11. "Wilfred Bohun stood rooted to the spot long enough to see the idiot go out into the sunshine, and even to see his dissolute brother hail him with a sort of <u>avuncular</u> jocularity."

The Innocence Of Father Brown by Gilbert K. Chesterton

(a) satiric   (b) senseless   (c) joking   (d) like an uncle
(e) without pretense

12. "Servile and fawning as he had been before, he was now as domineering and <u>bellicose</u>."

The Sea Wolf by Jack London

(a) hostile   (b) gleeful   (c) independent   (d) passive   (e) quiet

13. "Now and again he heard the singsong cadence of a Chinese quotation."

Kim by Rudyard Kipling

(a) rhyming pattern (b) rhythmic flow (c) vocabulary
(d) grammatical structure (e) moral

14. "Thus, like figs, do these doctrines fall for you, my friends: Imbibe now their juice and their sweet substance."

Thus Spake Zarathustra by Friedrich Nietzsche

(a) pour (b) spill (c) drink (d) drown (e) eat heartily

15. "Behind her, waiting their turn to name themselves to the Countess, Archer noticed a number of the recalcitrant couples who had declined to meet her at Mrs. Lovell Mingott's."

The Age of Innocence by Edith Wharton

(a) reclusive (b) unattractive (c) open, honest (d) resistant
(e) untruthful

16. "...They will be exposed to peculiar temptations, on account of the carnal desires which have heretofore subsisted between them."

From Twice Told Tales by Nathaniel Hawthorne

(a) unspoken (b) sexual (c) forbidden (d) unrealized (e) restraining

17. "'The Alchemist' castigates quackery and its foolish encouragers..."

A History of English Literature by Robert Huntington Fletcher

(a) criticizes (b) restrains (c) discourages (d) favors (e) embodies

18. "But I was determined to be discreet, to bear in mind my being only four months a widow, and to be as quiet as possible: and I have been so, my dear creature; I have admitted no one's attentions but Mainwaring's."

Lady Susan by Jane Austen

(a) invisible (b) accepted (c) friendly (d) outgoing (e) circumspect

19. "For the convenience of the reader I will recapitulate the incidents of those days in as exact a manner as possible."

The Mysterious Affair at Styles by Agatha Christie

(a) elaborate (b) memorize (c) write down (d) summarize (e) share

20. "For the helmet of Pluto, which maketh the politic man go invisible, is secrecy in the counsel, and <u>celerity</u> in the execution."

The Essays by Sir Francis Bacon

(a) security (b) deceit (c) swiftness (d) thoroughness (e) respect

21. "The moral I draw is that the writer should seek his reward in the pleasure of his work and in release from the burden of his thought; and, indifferent to aught else, care nothing for praise or <u>censure</u>, failure or success."

Moon and Sixpence by W. Somerset Maugham

(a) examination (b) criticism (c) support (d) exacerbation (e) suppression

22. "...as Queequeg was about to <u>precede</u> me up the stairs, the lady reached forth her arm, and demanded his harpoon; she allowed no harpoon in her chambers."

Moby Dick by Herman Melville

(a) go before (b) agree to (c) carry (d) trail (e) pull

23. "We are, nevertheless, seldom able with certainty to tell in any given species, at what period of life, or at what period of the year, or whether only at long intervals, the check falls; or, again, what is the <u>precise</u> nature of the check."

The Voyage of the Beagle by Charles Darwin

(a) aforementioned (b) perceived (c) exact (d) expected (e) intended

24. "Arms and the <u>clarion</u> for the battle, but the song of thanksgiving to the victory!"

The Last of The Mohicans by James Fenimore Cooper

(a) sword (b) trumpet (c) comprehensive (d) rations (e) armor

25. "This was the <u>cloister</u> of the nuns, and the old woman was the Abbess."

The Yellow Fairy Book by Andrew Lang

(a) religious ritual (b) perception (c) place for religious seclusion (d) home (e) group

Lesson IX

clin, clivus, cognit, collum, compl, copia, coquo, cord

CLIN	**CLIVUS**	**COGNIT**	**COLLUM**
to bend	slope	learn	neck

COMPL	**COPIA**	**COQUO**	**CORD**
to fill	plenty	to cook	heart

decline, inclination, inclined, recline, declivity, proclivity, cognition, cognizant, incognito, accolade, complement, complementary, comply, copious, concoct, precocious, accord, concord, concordance, cordial

Word Definitions

decline
v. to become smaller, fewer, or less; to decrease; to say no to
n. a continuous loss of strength, numbers, or value; a downward slope
"They declined the invitation because they were ill."
declinare to bend down, turn aside: *de-* down + *clinare* to bend

inclination
n. a tendency or urge to act or feel in a particular way; a slope
"A nature lover, he had an inclination toward outdoor sports like skiing and hiking."
inclinare to bend or lower

inclined
v. to be favorably disposed toward or willing to do; sloping or leaning
"I was not inclined to agree with his radical viewpoint."
inclinare to bend or lower

recline
v. to lean or lie back in a relaxed position
"Chairs are to sit in, beds to recline in."
reclinare to bend back, recline: *re-* back + *clinare* to bend

declivity
n. a downward slope
"The path had a steep declivity from the town to the seashore."
declivis sloping down: *de-* down + *clivus* a slope

proclivity	**n.** an inclination or predisposition "A sadist, he had a proclivity for inflicting pain." *proclivis* inclined: *pro-* forward + *clivus* slope
cognition	**n.** the mental action or process of acquiring knowledge through thought, experience, and the senses *cognitive (adj.)* "Cognition is the Latinate term for 'thinking.'" *cognoscere* to learn or recognize
cognizant	**adj.** fully informed; aware of "She was cognizant of her environment, but chose to ignore the dangers." *cognoscere* to learn or recognize
incognito	**adj. & adv.** with one's true identity concealed **n.** an assumed or false identity "To escape their fans, Hollywood stars often travel incognito." *in-* not, against + *cognoscere* to learn or recognize
accolade	**n.** something granted as a special honor or in recognition of merit; applause; a touch on the shoulder with a sword, or an embrace, that is part of the knighthood ceremony "The Nobel Prize for Literature is the highest literary accolade." *ad-* to, toward + *collum* neck
complement	**v.** to add something that enhances or improves (something else) **n.** a thing that adds to and completes something else; the opposite of something else (in a positive sense, like yin and yang) "Her vision and his patience with details complement each other perfectly." *complere* to fill up, finish, fulfill: *com-* (intensive force) + *plere* to fill
complementary	**adj.** combining in such a way as to form a complete whole or enhance each other; "Spaghetti and meatballs are complementary." *complere* to fill up, finish, fulfill: *com-* (intensive force) + *plere* to fill
comply	**v.** to act in accordance with a wish or command; to meet specified standards "Even the president must comply with the law." *complere* to fill up, finish, fulfill: *com-* (intensive force) + *plere* to fill
copious	**adj.** abundant in quantity or supply "A diligent student, he takes copious notes in class." *copia* plenty
concoct	**v.** to make by combining ingredients; to invent or devise a story or plan "The cocktail was concocted of three liqueurs plus orange juice." *concoction (n.)* *concoquere* to cook together: *con-* together + *coquere* to cook

LESSON IX CLIN, CLIVUS, COGNIT, COLLUM, COMPL, COPIA, COQUO, CORD

precocious   **adj.** demonstrating advanced abilities at an early age
"A precocious child's talent far exceeds age expectation."
praecoquere to ripen fully or early: *prae-* before + *coquere* to cook

accord   **v.** to give or grant someone power or recognition
n. an official agreement or treaty; a meeting of the minds (similar to concord)
"The war hero was accorded the Medal of Honor."
ad- to + *cor, cordis* heart, mind, or spirit

concord   **n.** an agreement, harmony; a treaty (similar to accord)
"The quarrel finally gave way to concord."
concors agreeing, harmonious: *con-* together + *cor, cordis* heart, mind, or spirit

concordance   **n.** agreement, consistency; an alphabetical list of the important words and their occurrence in a text, usually with citations of the passages concerned
"A concordance lists all uses of 'methinks' in Shakespeare."
concordare to agree; to go by a pattern: *con-* together + *cor, cordis* heart, mind, or spirit

cordial   **adj.** warm and friendly; strongly felt
n. a post-dinner liqueur
"The diplomat extended a cordial welcome to the guests."
cor-, cordis heart, mind, or spirit

Exercise A

Fill in the blanks in the sentences below with the correct form of a word in the scroll above.

1. Illustrations should _____ the author's text.

2. After a sterling performance, Jerome received high _____ from the critics.

3. Gorbachev, a former KGB agent, was _____ of the secret inner workings of the Soviet government and so was able to steer it toward reform.

4. Maria and Javier, although unable to stand each other's company since their divorce, were in _____ when it came to raising their children.

5. Upon meeting Donald Trump, Michael had to resist an _____ to tug on the tycoon's hair to determine whether or not Trump wore a toupee.

6. She was initially _____ to vote for Hillary Clinton in the Democratic primary, but changed her mind at the last minute and cast her ballot for Barack Obama.

7. Ricky's bicycle gained speed as he coasted down the _____, and Marcia became nervous that he would be unable to stop at the bottom.

8. Research on _____ has helped psychologists devise more effective strategies for helping patients with phobias, obsessive thinking, and depression.

9. James Bond, even though he is a spy, operates openly and rarely goes _____.

10. Britney wished she could _____ the invitation to the Hollywood gala, but her publicist said it was important for her to rehabilitate her image.

11. She studied public health because it was _____ to her work as a doctor in the inner city.

12. Although he is publicly _____ to the former Green Party candidate, privately Al Gore feels nothing but contempt for Ralph Nader.

13. The always unusual Barrymore family chose to eat on this occasion as the Romans once did; they _____ on couches and ate with their hands.

14. Chef Boyardee _____ a delicious soup out of common and inexpensive ingredients.

15. In the movie *The Sixth Sense*, a young boy has a natural _____ for talking with spirits.

16. The experimental data on the position of the sun measured by Galileo were in _____ with the theoretical values that he had already calculated.

17. The student council brokered a student code of behavior, helping the jocks and the "nerds" they liked to torment reach _____.

18. During his childhood, Mozart was recognized as a _____ musician.

19. The United States was asked to _____ with the Geneva Conventions on human rights during the invasion and occupation of Iraq.

20. He drank _____ amounts of water, but it did nothing to abate his hunger.

Exercise B

Match the word with the letter of its definition.

1. ___ accolade
2. ___ accord
3. ___ cognition
4. ___ cognizant
5. ___ complement
6. ___ complementary
7. ___ comply
8. ___ concoct
9. ___ concord
10. ___ concordance
11. ___ cordial
12. ___ copious
13. ___ decline
14. ___ declivity
15. ___ inclination
16. ___ incline
17. ___ incognito
18. ___ recline
19. ___ proclivity
20. ___ precocious

a) fully aware of, knowing
b) with one's true identity concealed
c) a commendation or award
d) plentiful, large (quantity)
e) to make by combining ingredients
f) a natural tendency toward something
g) an official agreement or treaty
h) to be favorably disposed (toward something)
i) a desire (to do something)
j) combining to form a complete whole
k) to lie back; to rest
l) a state of harmony, agreement
m) the process of acquiring knowledge; thought
n) to refuse politely
o) agreement; a type of literary index
p) warm and courteous
q) a downward slope
r) to follow a rule or command
s) to add to and enhance something else
t) demonstrating advanced abilities at an early age

Exercise C

Solve the crossword puzzle:

Across
3. the process of acquiring knowledge; thought
6. demonstrating advanced abilities at an early age
8. a commendation or award
9. plentiful, large (quantity)
10. to add to or enhance something else
11. fully aware; knowing
12. to refuse politely
13. warm and courteous
16. a natural tendency towards something
17. to lie back; to rest
18. a downward slope

Down
1. agreement a type of literary index
2. combing to form a whole
4. to desire (to do something)
5. to make by combining ingredients
7. to be favorably disposed (toward something)
9. to follow a rule or command
10. a state of harmony, agreement
14. with one's true identity concealed
15. an official agreement or treaty

Lesson X

corpor, cred/credit, cresc, cruc, cubo, culp, cupio

CORPOR **body**	***CRED, CREDIT*** **to believe**	***CRESC*** **to grow**	***CRUC*** **cross**
CUBO **to lie down**	***CULP*** **fault; guilt**	***CUPIO*** **to desire**	

corporal, corpse, corpulent, incorporate, creditable, credulity, creed, accrue, accumulate, crescendo, excrescence, cruciform, incumbent, incubus, recumbent, succumb, culpable, inculpate, covet, cupidity

Word Definitions

corporal
adj. relating to the body
"Flogging was the usual form of corporal punishment at sea."
corpus body

corpse
n. a dead body, especially human
"He stumbled across a decaying corpse while hiking in the backcountry."
corpus body

corpulent
adj. (of a person) fat; rotund
"A man of girth, Falstaff was a corpulent fellow."
corpus body

incorporate
v. to take in or include as part of a whole; to constitute as a legal corporation
adj. constituted as a legal corporation
"The two Andovers decided to incorporate as a single town."
incorporare to embody < *corpus* body

creditable
adj. deserving public acknowledgment, but not necessarily outstanding
"The applicant had a creditable but undistinguished work history."
credere to believe, to trust

credulity n. a disposition to trust o r believe too readily
"The outlandish alibi strained credulity."
credere to believe, to trust

creed n. a system of belief; a religious doctrine
"The creed of the jungle is kill or be killed."
credere to believe, to trust

accrue v. (of a benefit or sum of money) to grow through regular increases or additions
"Over the years, a savings bond accrues annual interest."
accrual (n.)
accrescere to grow: *ad-* to + *crescere* to grow

accumulate v. to gather together a number or quantity of
"The clouds accumulated, darkened, and loosed a rainstorm."
accumulatory (adj.)
accumulare to heap up: *ad-* to + *cumulare* to increase, pile up

crescendo n. a gradual increase in volume in a piece of music; the peak of such loudness
"'The 1812 Overture' ends with a crescendo of cannons and bells."
crescere to grow, to increase

excrescence n. an abnormal outgrowth on a body or plant; an unattractive or superfluous addition or feature
"A wart is an unsightly excrescence."
excrescere to grow out or up: *ex-* out + *crescere* to grow

cruciform adj. having the shape of a cross
"The ankh is a looped, cruciform Egyptian symbol of life."
crux, cruc- cross + *forma* shape

incumbent adj. required of (someone) as a duty or responsibility
n. the current holder of a post or elective office
"It is incumbent upon a soldier to obey the orders of a superior."
incumbere to lean forward; to press on < *cubare* to lie on

incubus n. a male demon believed to have sex with sleeping women; a nightmare
"Hieronymus Bosch painted hellish scenes of devils and incubi."
in- against + *cubare* to lie on

recumbent adj. lying down
"The model was recumbent on Matisse's sofa."
recumbere to recline, lie back: *re-* back + *cubare* to lie on

succumb v. to fail to resist (pleasure, temptation, etc.); to die from the effect of a disease or injury; to yield or to give in to
"Eve succumbed to the serpent's suggestion to eat forbidden fruit."
succumbere to collapse or surrender: *sub-* under + *cubare* to lie

culpable adj. deserving blame; guilty
"Pamela Smart was culpable in her husband's murder, even though she

	persuaded her teenage lover to shoot him."
	culpability (n.)
	culpare to blame
inculpate	**v.** to accuse, blame, or incriminate
	"The witness <u>inculpated</u> the suspect."
	inculpation (n.)
	inculpare to blame, find fault with: *in-* against + *culpare* to blame
covet	**v.** to yearn to possess (something belonging to someone else); to desire strongly
	"His fiancée <u>coveted</u> the engagement ring in the shop window."
	cupere to desire
cupidity	**n.** greed for money or possessions
	"King Midas's name is synonymous with <u>cupidity</u>."
	cupere to desire

Exercise A

Fill in the blanks in the sentences below with the correct form of a word in the scroll above.

1. The _____ dog struggled to support its weight on its skinny legs.

2. To capture the attention of the class, the math teacher sought to _____ rap music in his multimedia presentation of integrals.

3. According to modern behaviorists, _____ punishment is ineffective, harms children's self-esteem, and can lead to bullying.

4. "Practice makes perfect" is the personal _____ of Jerry Rice, perhaps the greatest football player ever to grace the gridiron.

5. Until he discovered an old IBM stock certificate in his attic, Enrique did not fully appreciate how an investment could _____ value over time.

6. In *Gimpel the Fool* by I.B. Singer, everyone in town takes advantage of Gimpel's _____, until he discovers the entire town has been lying to him.

7. In *Scent of a Woman*, Chris O'Donnell's character is loyal to those he believes to be his friends and refuses to _____ them.

8. The Egyptians were able to preserve the _____ of their pharaohs by mummifying their remains.

9. He did a _____ job on the project, but didn't live up to my high expectations.

10. No man could resist _____ to the siren's call, despite its portent of doom.

11. Mr. Wilson held his neighbors _____ for all the damage done to his lawn and home by their irrepressible son, Dennis the Menace.

12. Freud felt his patients would be more relaxed and inclined to reveal themselves during analysis if they were _____ on a sofa that faced away from him.

13. Most Christian churches are in a _____ shape.

14. To _____ the possessions of another can only lead to disillusionment and unhappiness; it's best to be happy with what one has.

15. Ravel's "Bolero" is one long _____, from beginning to end.

16. Medusa had an _____ so frightening that the mere sight of it turned men to stone: live snakes growing from her head in place of hair.

17. The image of the _____ haunted the film's audience members and led many to suffer nightmares.

18. The stockbroker's _____ eventually led him to steal from his clients.

19. After several moves, the couple tried to not _____ so much junk.

20. The _____ mayor had two years remaining in his term.

Exercise B

Match the word with the letter of its definition.

1. ___ accrue
2. ___ accumulate
3. ___ corporal
4. ___ corpse
5. ___ corpulent
6. ___ covet
7. ___ creditable
8. ___ credulity
9. ___ creed
10. ___ crescendo
11. ___ cruciform
12. ___ culpable
13. ___ cupidity
14. ___ excrescence
15. ___ incorporate
16. ___ inculpate
17. ___ incumbent
18. ___ incubus
19. ___ recumbent
20. ___ succumb

a) shaped like a cross
b) exceedingly fat
c) a system of beliefs
d) to yield to; to fall prey to
e) pertaining to the body
f) an abnormal growth
g) deserving of public acknowledgment, but not necessarily successful or outstanding
h) a steady increase in volume (in music)
i) a dead body
j) reclining, in a resting position
k) a tendency to believe too readily
l) to grow or increase through additions
m) to include in a preexisting whole
n) the holder of a post or elective office
o) to accuse or blame
p) greed
q) to yearn to possess something
r) deserving blame
s) to gather together a number or quantity
t) a male demon

Exercise C

Solve the crossword puzzle:

Across
3. A gradual increase in volume in a piece of music. 5. A dead body, especially human. 6. A system of belief; a religious doctrine. 7. (of a person) Fat. 8. To fail to resist (pleasure, temptation, etc.); to die from a disease or injury. 12. To accuse, blame, or incriminate. 15. Greed for money or possessions. 16. To yearn to possess (something belonging to someone else). 17. Required of (someone) as a duty or responsibility. 19. Lying down. 20. To gather together a number or quantity of (something).

Down
1. To take in or include as part of a whole; to constitute as a legal corporation. 2. Relating to the body. 4. A disposition to trust too readily; gullibility. 9. Deserving acknowledgment, but not necessarily outstanding or successful. 10. Guilty, deserving blame. 11. A male demon believed to have sex with sleeping women; a nightmare. 13. Having the shape of a cross. 14. An abnormal outgrowth on a body or plant; an unattractive or superfluous addition or feature. 18. (Of a benefit or sum of money) received in regular or increasing amounts.

Lesson XI

curr/curs, da/dat, dent, dextra, divin, doc/doct

CURR, CURS
to run

DA, DAT
to give

DENT
tooth

DEXTRA
right hand

DIVIN
divine

DOC, DOCT
to teach; lead

concur, concurrent, curriculum, cursory, discourse, excursion, incur, incursion, precursor, succor, data, mandate, indentation, trident ambidextrous, deify, deity, divine, divinity, docile

Word Definitions

concur
: **v.** to agree; to happen at the same time
"We can't begin until all parties concur on the plan."
concurrence (n.)
concurrere to run together or agree: *con-* together + *currere* to run

concurrent
: **adj.** existing or happening at the same time
"Concurrent jail terms are served simultaneously."
concurrere to run together or agree: *con-* together + *currere* to run

curriculum
: **n.** the subjects comprising a course of study in a school or college
"The pre-med curriculum is very challenging."
curricular (adj.)
curriculum race course or racing chariot; course of action

cursory
: **adj.** hasty and therefore not thorough; superficial
"The restaurant inspection was cursory, and the health officer failed to notice the mouse droppings."
cursoriness (n.)
cursorius of a runner < *cursor* runner; chariot racer; courier

discourse	**v.** to speak or write authoritatively about a subject **n.** formal discussion "Darwin wrote a detailed discourse on finches." *discurrere* to run around: *dis-* apart, down from + *currere* to run
excursion	**n.** a short journey, especially taken for leisure "Tomorrow, let's make an excursion to the lake." *excurrere* to run out: *ex-* out + *currere* to run
incur	**v.** to earn as a result of one's actions "Sloppy workmanship incurred the wrath of the boss." *incurrere*: *in-* toward + *currere* to run
incursion	**n.** an invasion or attack; overstepping of a boundary or limit "Navy Seals made a nighttime incursion onto the enemy's beach." *incurrere*: *in-* toward + *currere* to run
precursor	**n.** something that comes before and leads to a similar thing "The Pony Express was the precursor of the modern postal service." *praecurrere* to run before, anticipate: *prae-* before + *currere* to run
succor	**n.** aid or emotional support in times of hardship and distress **v.** to render assistance; to provide relief "The Red Cross provides succor to disaster victims." *succurrere* to run to the aid of : *sub-* under, up to + *currere* to run
data	**n.** facts, statistics, and other items of information "His experiment did not yield enough data to draw meaningful conclusions." *datum* something given < *dare* to give
mandate	**v.** to require (something) or give (someone) authority to do something **n.** an official order or commission to do something "Hospital policy mandates that instruments be sterilized." *mandare* to commission or command: *manus* hand + *dare* to give
indentation	**n.** the action of indenting or the state of being indented; setting inward from the margin "A small indentation marked where the BB had hit the car." *indentare*: *en-*, *in-* into + *dens, dentis* tooth
trident	**n.** a three-pronged spear "Some gladiators used the trident and net as weapons." *tri-* three + *dens, dentis* tooth
ambidextrous	**adj.** able to use the right and left hand equally well "An ambidextrous batter can hit both right-handed and left-handed." *ambi-* both, two + *dexter* right (side); skill
deify	**v.** to make into or worship as a god "Alexander was deified and worshiped by the Egyptians." *deus* god

deity   **n.** a god or goddess; the creator or supreme being
"The <u>deity</u> Zeus was known for his promiscuity."
deus god

divine   **v.** to discover by guesswork or intuition; to have supernatural insight into the future
adj. devoted to God, sacred
"A <u>divining</u> rod is a forked rod that supposedly can find underground sources of water."
divus godlike

divinity   **n.** the state or quality of being divine; the study of theology
"A theological seminary is also known as a <u>divinity</u> school."
divus godlike

docile   **adj.** ready to accept control or instruction; submissive
"Domesticated animals are <u>docile</u> descendants of wild animals."
docere to teach

Exercise A

Fill in the blanks in the sentences below with the correct form of a word in the scroll above.

1. Sadly, many people confuse the wickedness of the devil's pitchfork with the splendor of Poseidon's _____.

2. The Secret Service would not have permitted President Clinton to make the occasional _____ to a McDonald's had he been in office after Sept. 11, 2001.

3. It's a dire mistake to confuse a feral wolf with a _____ husky.

4. The foolhardy hiker would _____ great danger by attempting to climb Mount Washington alone during the middle of the winter.

5. Coach Bill Parcells' _____ that his players treat him and his staff with respect bordering on reverence was disobeyed at the player's risk.

6. The fire official's _____ inspection of the decrepit apartment building came under fire after the building burned down.

7. Carter Beauford, the percussionist of the Dave Matthews Band, is _____, so he can play drums with both hands equally well.

8. People who spontaneously took food, clothing, medical supplies, and bottled water to New Orleans after Hurricane Katrina brought _____ to thousands.

9. MCAS tests, required for high school graduation, are part an attempt to standardize the _____ of Massachusetts public schools.

10. Conflict between the northern and southern states about the moral legitimacy of slavery was a _____ to the Civil War.

11. Although Steven Hawking was fascinated by Homer Simpson's idea of a doughnut-shaped universe, Simpson had no _____ to support his claim.

12. At Hogwart's, Hermione was more inclined to bookish study and reasoned _____, while Ron and Harry preferred learning by trial and error.

13. It is rare for everyone to _____ with the president's policies, but most members of his party go along in exchange for his support of their pet projects.

14. The _____ of ancient Rome were very human in their mix of virtues and failings.

15. Because of their belief in Quetzalcoatl, the white snake god, some Aztecs _____ Cortez when the pale-skinned Spaniard arrived in Mesoamerica.

16. An _____ and a new paragraph should be used in written dialogue every time the speaker changes.

17. The rulers of most ancient civilizations claimed _____ and cemented their authority through religious ceremonies and pronouncements.

18. He was given five to 10 years for assault and seven to 14 years for attempted kidnapping, but his sentences were _____, so he was eligible for parole after serving seven years.

19. If Andrew was to pass his math exam, there had to be some _____ intervention.

20. Prior to the _____ into the neighboring country, the mighty forces checked their weapons and awaited instructions.

LESSON XI CURR/CURS, DA/DAT, DENT, DEXTRA, DIVIN, DOC/DOCT

Exercise B

Match the word with the letter of its definition.

1. ___ ambidextrous
2. ___ concur
3. ___ concurrent
4. ___ curriculum
5. ___ cursory
6. ___ data
7. ___ deify
8. ___ deity
9. ___ discourse
10. ___ divine
11. ___ divinity
12. ___ docile
13. ___ excursion
14. ___ incur
15. ___ incursion
16. ___ indentation
17. ___ mandate
18. ___ precursor
19. ___ succor
20. ___ trident

a) to treat or worship as a god
b) a demand or instruction for action
c) easily managed, well behaved
d) the quality of godliness
e) the classes comprising a course of study
f) a staff with three tines or prongs
g) performed quickly without attention to detail
h) sacred
i) assistance provided during a time of hardship
j) to agree
k) to bring upon one's self
l) a brief trip designed for pleasure
m) the action of indenting
n) a god or goddess
o) something that precedes
p) equally skilled with both hands
q) pieces of information, used for analysis
r) existing or happening at the same time
s) to speak or write authoritatively about a subject
t) an invasion or attack

Exercise C

Solve the crossword puzzle.

Across
4. To bring upon oneself through one's own actions. 9. Something giving someone the authority to do certain things. 11. Assistance and support in times of hardship and distress. 12. Hasty and therefore not thorough. 13. A person or thing that comes before another similar person or thing. 15. Existing or happening at the same time. 16. Submissive, gentle. 18. The state or quality of being divine; theology. 19. A three-pronged spear, especially as an attribute of Poseidon (Neptune).

Down
1. The classes comprising a course of study in a school or college. 2. Able to use the right and left hand equally well. 3. The action of indenting or the state of being indented. 5. To speak or write authoritatively about a subject. 6. To agree. 7. An invasion 8. Statistics used for reference or analysis. 10. A short journey, especially taken for leisure. 14. To make into or worship as a god. 16. A god or goddess; the creator or supreme being. 17. To discover by guesswork or intuition; to have supernatural insight into the future.

Lesson XII
dict, doleo, domin

DICT-
to say

DOLEO-
to grieve

DOMIN-
to rule

benediction, dictator, diction, dictum, ditty, edict, interdiction, jurisdiction, malediction, valediction, verdict, condole, condolence, domain, domestic, domicile, dominant, dominate, domineer, dominion

Word Definitions

benediction n. the utterance or bestowing of a blessing
"The priest usually pronounces a <u>benediction</u> at the end of Mass."
benedicere to bless: *bene* well + *dicere* to say

dictator n. a ruler with total power over a country or institution
"Hitler became a <u>dictator</u> after suspending most democratic rights."
dictare to dictate

diction n. the choice and use of words in speech or writing; enunciation
"When writing a formal essay, it is important to remember not to use colloquial <u>diction</u>."
dicere to say

dictum n. an authoritative pronouncement; a saying (pl. is *dicta*)
"According to royal <u>dictum</u>, July 14th became known as 'King Phillip's Day.'"
dicere to say

ditty n. a short, simple song
"'What do ya do with a drunken sailor?' is a <u>ditty</u>."
dictare to dictate

edict	**n.** an official order or proclamation; a decree "The Wannsee edict condemned all Jews to extermination." *edictal (adj.)* *edicere: e-* out + *dicere* to say, to tell
interdiction	**n.** a prohibition "Customs agents attempt interdiction of illegal drugs to the US." *interdict (v.)* *interdicere* to forbid by decree: *inter-* between + *dicere* to say, to tell
jurisdiction	**n.** the official power to make legal decisions and judgments "Though not a state, Puerto Rico falls under U.S. jurisdiction." *jurisdictal (adj.)* *jurisdictio*: legal system: *juris-* law, court + *dictio* declaration < *dicere* to say
malediction	**n.** a curse; swear word or phrase; slander "'Damn him to hell' was a stronger malediction when most people believed in God and the devil." *maledicere* to speak evil of: *mal-* evil + *dicere* to say, to tell
valediction	**n.** the act of saying farewell; a valedictory speech "'May we fare well!' was the graduation speaker's valediction." *vale* goodbye + *dicere* to say
verdict	**n.** a final decision on the facts in a civil or criminal case or an inquest "A jury is charged to render a verdict of guilt or innocence." *verus* true + *dictum* saying
condole	**v.** to express sympathy for "The mourners at the funeral condoled the recent widow." *condolere* to suffer with another: *con-* with + *dolere* to grieve, suffer
condolence	**n.** an expression of sympathy "The pastor paid a condolence visit to the family of the departed." *condolere* to suffer with another: *con-* with + *dolere* to grieve, suffer
domain	**n.** an area owned or controlled by a ruler or government; area of action or influence "The Mongols' domain extended from present-day China to Hungary." *dominus* lord, master (of the house)
domestic	**adj.** relating to a home or family affairs or relations; a household servant; tame, as of animals "Cooking and sewing were once necessary domestic skills for women." *domus* house
domicile	**n.** the country in which a person has permanent residence; the residence itself "In law, one's domicile denotes one's primary place of residence." *domus* home

LESSON XII DICT, DOLEO, DOMIN

dominant   **adj.** most important, powerful, or influential
"The brain's left hemisphere is <u>dominant</u> in language activity."
dominare to rule or govern < *dominus* lord, master

dominate   **v.** to have a commanding or controlling influence over
"For decades, the Yankees <u>dominated</u> the American League."
dominare to rule or govern < *dominus* lord, master

domineer   **v.** to behave in an arrogant and overbearing way
"A <u>domineering</u> person insists that everyone do things her way."
dominare to rule or govern < *dominus* lord, master

dominion   **n.** sovereignty; area under control
"A lion's <u>dominion</u> extends to 100 acres or more."
dominus lord, master

Exercise A

Fill in the blanks in the sentences with the correct form of a word in the scroll above.

1. Amelia Earhart defied the _____ expectations for women of her era, instead setting records for solo flight.

2. The manager at Dairy Queen had a simple _____ she used to discourage unprofessional conduct by her workers: "Save the drama for your mama."

3. The legality of capital punishment is under the _____ of the individual states, but the legality of early-term abortion is controlled by the federal government.

4. While the legal powers of the royal family have been supplanted by a parliamentary government, the British Isles are still considered the queen's _____.

5. In the years since the collapse of the Soviet Union, the United States has become the _____ nation in international relations and conflict resolution.

6. Young writing students sometimes over-use imagery and metaphor while ignoring _____, the most powerful tool a writer has in setting a tone.

7. During Prohibition, all alcoholic beverages were under a strict _____, but my grandparents made "bathtub gin" for parties out of grain alcohol and flavorings.

8. Although Charlie Brown was the captain of the baseball team, it was the _____ Lucy who told everyone what to do.

9. Kobe Bryant's reputation will be forever tainted by the sex scandal in Colorado, regardless of the _____ reached by the jury in his trial.

10. The Patriots managed to _____ the Buffalo Bills in the final game of the regular season, despite their earlier loss to the Bills.

11. According to the Biblical book of Exodus, Moses escaped the Egyptian _____ that every Jewish male child be slaughtered.

12. As Buffy the vampire slayer went off to defend Sunnydale from impending doom, her friend Willow pronounced a _____ on the demons in the town.

13. Fidel Castro, the former _____ of Cuba, openly aided the Soviet Union and its satellites during the cold war.

14. Mitt Romney has a vacation home in New Hampshire, but his residence in Massachusetts is his legal _____ , where he votes.

15. The _____ for the graduating class was quite emotional, as several graduates had enlisted and were heading to Iraq or Afghanistan after basic training.

16. While on her way to her grandmother's house, Little Red Riding Hood hummed a _____ her mother often sang to her.

17. When her teacher's mother died, the student sent her a note of _____.

18. At the end of the service, the priest offered a _____.

19. The Romans exercised _____ over vast territories of present-day Europe, including modern-day England.

20. Her husband's co-workers all _____ the widow after the funeral.

Exercise B

Match the word with the letter of its definition.

1. ___ benediction
2. ___ condole
3. ___ condolence
4. ___ dictator
5. ___ diction
6. ___ dictum
7. ___ ditty
8. ___ domain
9. ___ domestic
10. ___ domicile
11. ___ dominant
12. ___ dominate
13. ___ domineer
14. ___ dominion
15. ___ edict
16. ___ interdiction
17. ___ jurisdiction
18. ___ malediction
19. ___ valediction
20. ___ verdict

a) a dwelling; a home
b) a short and simple song
c) to rule over or control; to tyrannize
d) a formal ruling or decree
e) pertaining to the home
f) to show sympathy or sorrow for another
g) area under legal authority of a court or governing body
h) enunciation; choice of words
i) powerful and influential; controlling
j) a prohibition
k) the decision of a jury
l) field of action or influence; a territory under a single ruler or government
m) sovereignty; area under control
n) an authoritative statement; a saying
o) a curse
p) the act of saying goodbye; a farewell
q) to prevail over; to hold power over
r) a single, all-powerful ruler
s) an expression of sympathy
t) a blessing

Exercise C

Solve the crossword puzzle.

Across
2. A ruler with total power over a county.
6. Relating to a home or family affairs; tame (animals).
9. A formal announcement; a saying.
10. The act of saying farewell.
12. The official power to make legal decisions and judgments.
14. A final decision on the facts in a court case.
16. Most important, controlling.
17. Expression of sympathy.
18. To behave in an arrogant and overbearing way.

Down
1. The bestowing of a blessing.
2. A short, simple song.
3. To have influence over.
4. An official order; a decree.
5. A prohibition.
7. A curse.
8. An area owned or controlled by a ruler or government.
9. Sovereignty.
11. Country of permanent residence.
13. Choice and use of words in speech or writing.
15. To express sympathy for.

Lesson XIII
domit, dormio, dorsum, duc/duct, ego, equ, err

DOMIT	DORMIO	DORSUM	DUC, DUCT
to tame	to sleep	back	to lead

EGO	EQU	ERR	
I	equal	to wander	

daunt, dauntless, indomitable, dormant, dorsal, endorse, aqueduct, deduce, induce, traduce, viaduct, egocentric, egotist, equal, equity, aberration, errant, erratic, erroneous, error

Word Definitions

daunt
v. to intimidate, make difficult
"The complex college admissions process is <u>daunting</u> to many."
daunting (adj.)
domare, domitare to tame, subdue, conquer

dauntless
adj. fearless and determined
"Outnumbered and out-gunned, the <u>dauntless</u> soldiers stood their ground."
domare, domitare to tame, subdue, conquer

indomitable
adj. impossible to subdue or defeat
"Helen Keller's <u>indomitable</u> spirit helped her overcome multiple disabilities."
in- not + *domitare* to tame, subdue, conquer

dormant
adj. in or seeming to be in a deep sleep; inactive
"A long <u>dormant</u> affection for the girl next door finally awakened when he reached adulthood."
domire to sleep

dorsal	*adj.* relating to the upper side of back (compare with ventral) "Sharks are known for their prominent, triangular dorsal fins." *dorsum* back
endorse	*v.* to declare one's public approval of; to sign a check on the back "Sports celebrities are paid millions to endorse and promote athletic products." *endorsement (n.)* *in-* on, upon + *dorsum* back
aqueduct	*n.* a bridge or viaduct carrying water over a valley or other gap "The Romans' stone aqueducts transported water from the mountains to cities." *aquae ductus* conduit: *aquae* water + *ducere* to lead
deduce	*v.* to arrive at by reasoning "Through experiment, Galileo was able to deduce the law of acceleration." *deduction (n.)* *deducere*: deduce, lead in: *de-* down + *ducere* to lead
induce	*v.* to succeed in persuading or leading someone to do something; to cause a condition "The physician induced labor two weeks after the mother's due date." *induction (n.)* *inducere* to lead in: *in-* in + *ducere* to lead
traduce	*v.* to speak badly of; to defame; to ridicule "'Mad' magazine satirically traduces conservative and liberal politicians alike." *traducement (n.)* *traducere* to parade past others: *trans-* across + *ducere* to lead
viaduct	*n.* a long bridge-like structure, typically a series of arches, carrying a road or railway across a valley or other low ground "While aqueducts carry water, viaducts are raised roadways." *via* road, way, journey + *ducere* to lead
egocentric	*adj.* Self-centered "He who acts as if the world revolves around himself is egocentric." *egocentricity (n.)* *ego* I + *kentron* (Greek for center)
egotist	*n.* a person who is very conceited or self-absorbed "A humble or self-deprecating person is the opposite of an egotist." *egotistical (adj.)* *ego* I
equal	*adj.* being the same in quantity, size, degree, value, or status *n.* a person or thing that is equal to another "As a piano virtuoso, Mozart had no equal." *equality (n.)* *aequus* even, level, equal

LESSON XIII DOMIT, DORMIO, DORSUM, DUC/DUCT, EGO, EQU, ERR

equity
n. fairness and impartiality; the value of shares issued by a company; value of a property or asset minus any debts against it
"The judge was known for his equity in commercial disputes."
aequitas justice, impartiality < *aequus* equal

aberration
n. an unwelcome deviation from what is normal
"The 'F' on the otherwise straight-'A' student's record was an aberration."
aberrare to stray from: *ab-* away from + *errare* to wander; to err

errant
adj. deviating from an accepted course or standards; misguided; wandering
"He was chided as errant for failing to follow company policy."
errare to wander; to err

erratic
adj. uneven or irregular in pattern or movement
"A performance that is not consistent and predictable is erratic."
errare to wander; to err

erroneous
adj. wrong, incorrect
"His logic was faulty, so his conclusions were erroneous."
errare to wander; to err

error
n. a mistake
"Edison's light filament resulted from much trial and error."
errare to wander; to err

Exercise A

Fill in the blanks in the sentences below with the correct form of a word in the scroll above.

1. The law clerk was required to do research for three junior partners, but where others had been crushed under the workload, he proved _____.

2. Celebrity athletes often become hopelessly _____ and act as if others exist only to flatter and serve them.

3. McDonald's and Burger King are an _____ distance from our home, but we usually go to the "home of the whopper" because there's less traffic that way.

4. She treated her children with _____ in her will.

5. When an orca, or "killer whale," is held in captivity for too long, its _____ fin begins to curl.

6. John Kerry _____ Barack Obama over Hillary Clinton in the Democratic presidential primary race.

85

7. *CSI*, the highly rated television show, follows forensic investigators and medical examiners as they _____ how and why crimes were committed.

8. Conservatives claim that Michael Moore's *Fahrenheit 9/11* was merely a brazen attempt by the activist director to _____ the president.

9. Brad belatedly realized that he'd scheduled dates with two different women on the same night, and quickly went to work trying to rectify the _____.

10. Martin Luther King Jr. did not allow the color of his skin to _____ or discourage him.

11. I don't know why he threw a tantrum: He's usually very well-behaved and yesterday's behavior was an _____.

12. The city of Pompeii was built at the base of Mount Vesuvius, which had been considered _____, but suddenly erupted after decades of inactivity.

13. Mrs. Henshaw tried to _____ her fourth grade class to recycle at home by making recycling a class project.

14. *Thomas the Tank Engine*, a popular children's television series, depicted the daily life of a little steam engine, chugging his way through tunnels and over _____.

15. Addiction to drugs can cause _____ and even criminal behavior by teenagers.

16. The _____ comings and goings of the neighbors caused much consternation and suspicion in the village.

17. The *New York Post* published an _____ report that John Kerry had chosen Dick Gephardt as his vice-presidential running mate.

18. "Trophy wives" and playgirls help perpetuate a culture in which it is acceptable for men to be inconsiderate _____, as long as they are wealthy.

19. The Romans built water-supplying _____, elaborate baths and public waterworks.

20. The _____ three musketeers and D'Artagnan battled and defeated many foes.

Exercise B

Match the word with the letter of its definition.

1. ___ aberration
2. ___ aqueduct
3. ___ daunt
4. ___ dauntless
5. ___ deduce
6. ___ dormant
7. ___ dorsal
8. ___ egocentric
9. ___ egotist
10. ___ equal
11. ___ endorse
12. ___ equity
13. ___ errant
14. ___ erratic
15. ___ erroneous
16. ___ error
17. ___ indomitable
18. ___ induce
19. ___ traduce
20. ___ viaduct

a) the quality of being fair and impartial
b) to intimidate or discourage
c) a bridge supported by a series of arches
d) a mistake
e) pertaining to the back of a person or animal
f) fearless and determined
g) asleep or inactive
h) misguided
i) to lead to by influence or persuasion
j) considering only one's own needs
k) unbeatable
l) a conceited and self-centered person
m) to conclude through logical reasoning
n) a structure designed to transport water
o) unsteady, irregular
p) of the same amount or value
q) to give public support to
r) incorrect
s) to humiliate or ridicule
t) an unwelcome deviation from the norm

Exercise C

Solve the crossword puzzle.

Across:
2. Of the upper side of back 4. To declare one's public approval of. 6. A bridge carrying a waterway over a valley 8. To discourage or intimidate. 12. Being the same in quantity, size, etc. 13. Impossible to subdue. 15. Self-centered. 16. Wrong. 17. Fearless and determined.

Down : 1. Misguided; deviating from an accepted course or standards. 3. An unwelcome deviation from what is normal. 5. To arrive at by reasoning. 7. A person who is excessively conceited or self-absorbed. 8. In a deep sleep; inactive. 9. To ridicule or slander. 10. A long bridge, typically a series of arches, carrying a road or railway across a valley or depression. 11. To persuade or lead someone to do something. 12. Uneven or irregular in pattern or movement. 14. A mistake. 15. The quality of being fair and impartial.

Lesson XIV

f a c / f i c / f e c / f e c t ,   f a c i e s ,   f a r i ,   f a l l / f a l s ,   f e r v

FAC, FIC, FEC, FECT
to make; to do

FACIES
face

FARI
to speak

FALL, FALS
to deceive

FERV
to boil

affect, facile, facsimile, fetish, fiction, mollify, rectify, deface, efface, façade, facet, fallacious, fallacy, falsify, infallible, affable, ineffable, effervescent, fervent, fervor

Word Definitions

affect
v. to have an impact or influence on; to pretend to have or feel
n. an emotion or desire as influencing behavior
"The death of my grandmother <u>affected</u> me more than the passing of my dog."
afficere to influence: *ad-* toward, to + *facere* to do, to make

facile
adj. ignoring the complexities of an issue; superficial; too easy
"Politicians frequently give <u>facile</u> answers to complex questions."
facilis easy to do

facsimile
n. an exact copy of written or printed matter
"A fax machine scans documents and transmits their <u>facsimiles</u> to a distant machine."
facere to do, to make + *similis* like

fetish
n. an inanimate object worshiped for its supposed magical powers; an unhealthy obsession with a particular object
"The old man had a <u>fetish</u> for rabbit's foot keychains, which he believed made him lucky and impervious to harm."
facere to do, to make

fiction	**n.** prose literature, especially novels; a thing that is invented, untrue "Investigation proved the senator's claim of military service to be a fiction." *fictitious (adj.)* *fingere* to form, contrive
mollify	**v.** to appease the anger or anxiety of "Nothing I could do or say seemed to mollify my mother." *mollification (n.)* *mollis* soft + *facere* to make
rectify	**v.** to put right, to correct "The accountant was able to rectify the computational error and balance the books." *rectification (n.)* *rectus* right + *facere* to make
deface	**v.** to spoil the surface or appearance of; to mar or disfigure "The vandals defaced the gravestones with red spray paint." *de-* (expressing reversal) + *face* face
efface	**v.** to erase from (memory, a surface) "Those who suffered in the concentration camp wanted to efface their horrible memories." *ex-* away, from + *face* face
façade	**n.** the (decorative) front of a building, facing onto the street or open space; a deceptive outward appearance "The smile was a façade that masked his deep sorrow." *face* face
facet	**n.** one side of something that is many-sided (as in a crystal); an aspect or feature "There are many facets to a well-cut diamond." *face* face
fallacy	**n.** a mistaken belief "It is a fallacy to presume that when one event follows another in time, they are cause and effect." *fallere* to deceive
fallacious	**adj.** containing or based on an error; tending to mislead "Since his facts and logic were both faulty, his argument was fallacious." *fallere* to deceive
falsify	**v.** to alter so as to mislead; to make false "A falsified signature on a check is grounds for imprisonment." *falsification (n.)* *falsifacere* falsify: *falsus* false + *facere* to make (variant of facere)
infallible	**adj.** incapable of making mistakes or being wrong; never failing "Catholics believe the Pope is infallible because his pronouncements are

LESSON XIV FAC/FIC/FEC/FECT, FACIES, FARI, FALL/FALS, FERV

inspired by God."
infallibility (n.)
in- not + *fallere* to deceive

affable **adj.** good-natured and sociable
"The new roommate proved <u>affable</u> and we quickly became friends."
affability (n.)
affari to speak to, to address: *ad-* to + *fari* to speak

ineffable **adj.** too great or sacred to be expressed in words
"His near-death experience was <u>ineffable</u>; he couldn't begin to describe it."
ineffability (n.)
in- not + *effari* to utter < *fari* to speak

effervescent **adj.** giving off bubbles, fizzy; vivacious and enthusiastic
"Marika had an <u>effervescent</u> personality that made her very popular."
effervescence (n.)
effervescere to boil up, to become excited: *ex-* out + *fervere* to boil

fervent **adj.** passionate; feverish
"John Brown was a <u>fervent</u> abolitionist whose beliefs led to violent deeds."
fervere to boil, to be hot

fervor **n.** an intense and passionate feeling
"Jonathan Edwards' <u>fervor</u> erupted in hell-fire sermons."
fervere to boil, to be hot

Exercise A

Fill in the blanks in the sentences below with the correct form of a word in the scroll above.

1. It is likely that a Sufi monk tried to _____ the magnificent sphinx around 1100 A.D., as an insult to the Egyptian people.

2. Although Bill Gates once boasted that Windows XP would be _____, it has proven to have as many bugs as its predecessors.

3. Richard Simmons is a _____ advocate of making weight loss fun, and his passion comes through in his dance videos.

4. Although Robin Hood wore a disguise to the archery contest, his expert marksmanship allowed the sheriff to see through the _____.

5. Although he was _____ , I couldn't help resenting his success.

6. The pacifier _____ the hungry baby – but only for a few minutes.

7. The gymnast's _____, bubbly presence helped her win the contest.

8. From design to management to advertising, Apple Computers excels in every _____ of the electronics business.

9. Justin Timberlake did not let the chorus of boos from the stadium crowd _____ his performance of the national anthem.

10. The _____ headline "Genetic Corn Potentially Deadly" did not accurately summarize the scientific research described in the newspaper article.

11. After a customer complained about the new software's buggy performance, the company quickly _____ the situation by issuing a patch.

12. *To Kill A Mockingbird* is considered one of the greatest pieces of American _____ , in part because the characters and plot are so realistic.

13. The _____ of the fans after the homecoming game victory spilled over into a celebration on the field and an impromptu parade around campus.

14. At first Henry seems smart, but most of his remarks are snarky and _____ , and most people quickly realize how shallow he is.

15. The teenager tried to _____ his age by tampering with his driver's license, but the bouncer spotted the fakery.

16. When she traveled across Europe, Judith kept a _____ of her passport tucked into a separate bag, in case she lost the original.

17. The _____ chemistry between the solo pianist and the orchestra conductor made for a sublime performance of Beethoven's piano concerto.

18. Felipe's _____ for women's shoes upset and embarrassed his wife.

19. The photographer was so good at _____ herself that often her subjects forgot she was there and stopped posing, allowing her to capture unselfconscious and intimate moments.

20. It is a _____ that developing more homes improves a town's finances: The cost of services such as schools, police, and roads for new residents invariably exceed the increase in property tax revenues.

Exercise B

Match the word with the letter of its definition.

1. ___ affable
2. ___ affect
3. ___ deface
4. ___ efface
5. ___ effervescent
6. ___ façade
7. ___ facet
8. ___ facile
9. ___ facsimile
10. ___ fallacious
11. ___ fallacy
12. ___ falsify
13. ___ fervent
14. ___ fervor
15. ___ fetish
16. ___ fiction
17. ___ ineffable
18. ___ infallible
19. ___ mollify
20. ___ rectify

a) to lie; to alter in a way that is false or misleading
b) an unhealthy obsession with an object; such an object
c) an illusion or front presented as truth
d) impossible to express; indescribable
e) easy; superficial
f) misleading, deceptive
g) to have an influence on
h) incapable of making mistakes; foolproof
i) to delete or erase
j) great intensity of emotion; passion
k) an exact duplicate or copy
l) one of many sides of an object
m) good-natured and easygoing; friendly
n) to correct or fix a problem
o) showing heightened passion or zeal
p) to calm, to appease
q) a prose story that is not factual
r) to ruin the surface of; to disfigure
s) full of life and vigor, bubbly in character
t) a mistake of belief or logic

Exercise C

Solve the crossword puzzle.

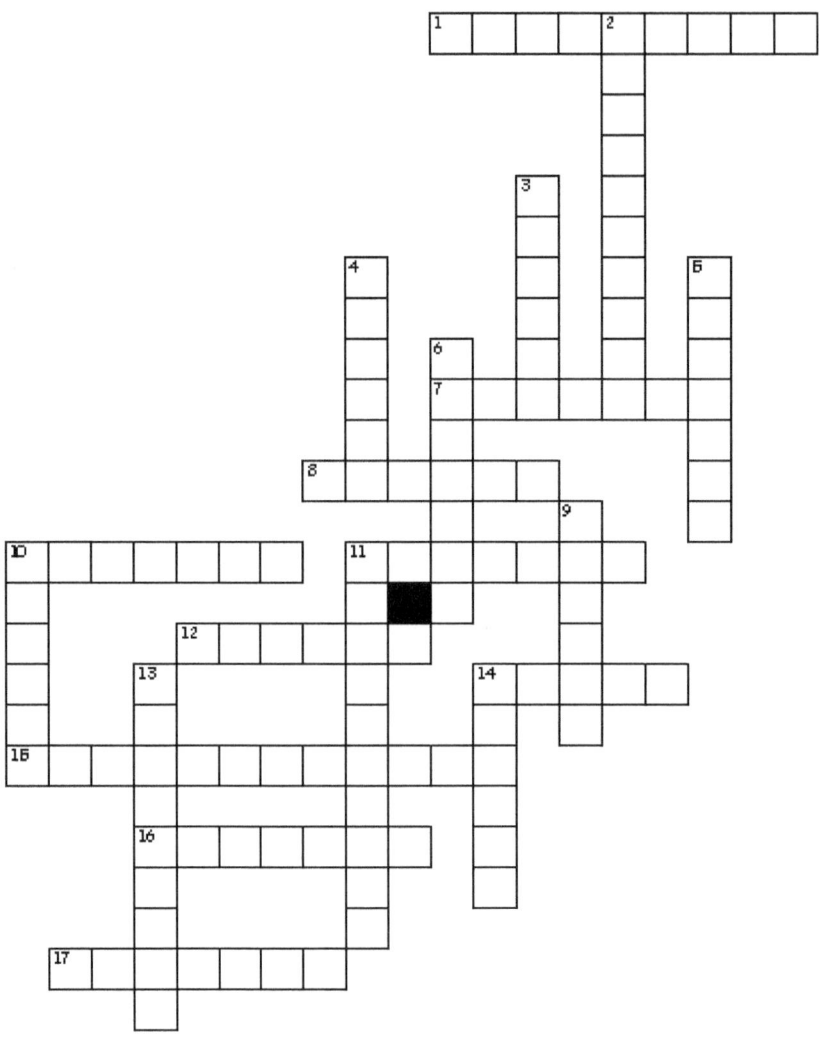

Across: 1. An exact copy of. 7. Intensely passionate. 8. To spoil the surface or appearance of. 10. A mistaken belief. 11. To alter so as to mislead. 12. Superficial; ignoring the complexities of an issue. 14. One side of something many-sided. 15. Giving off bubbles; enthusiastic. 16. A story that is invented or untrue. 17. To appease the anger or anxiety of.

Down: 2. Incapable of being wrong. 3. An intense and passionate feeling. 4. To erase or make disappear. 5. To correct. 6. Good-natured and sociable. 9. To change or influence. 10. The (ornamental) front of a building, facing the street; a deceptive outward appearance. 11. Containing or based on a fallacy; tending to mislead. 13. Too great or sacred to be expressed in words. 14. An inanimate object worshiped for its supposed magical powers.

Test 2

Choose the correct meaning for the underlined vocabulary word in each sentence.

1. "Adam eagerly opened the letter which had only just arrived, and conveyed a <u>cordial</u> invitation to stop with his grand-uncle at Lesser Hill, for as long a time as he could spare."

   The Lair of the White Worm by Bram Stoker

   (a) complimentary   (b) brief   (c) harmonious   (d) gracious   (e) lengthy

2. "Yet he was a guide of no mean order, who made up for the poverty of what he had to show by a <u>copious</u>, imaginative commentary."

   Tales and Fantasies by Robert Louis Stevenson

   (a) enhanced   (b) informed   (c) plentiful   (d) complementary   (e) devised

3. "I appear <u>incognito</u> of course, as you may gather from my appearance."

   The Four Million by O. Henry

   (a) disguised   (b) angry   (c) aware   (d) thoughtful   (e) larger than life

4. "But with the self-combating <u>proclivity</u> of the supersensitive, an answer thereto arose in Clare's own mind, and he almost feared it."

   Tess of the d'Urbervilles by Thomas Hardy

   (a) slope   (b) unnatural ability   (c) loss of strength   (d) tendency   (e) relaxation

5. "'I flatter myself I'm a "gentleman growed" as Peggotty said of David, and when you see Amy, you'll find her rather a <u>precocious</u> infant,' said Laurie, looking amused at her maternal air."

   Little Women by Louisa May Alcott

   (a) abundant   (b) mature   (c) wish or command   (d) enhanced   (e) fulfilling

6. "The information may be of use to you, if only to prevent your <u>credulity</u>, in judging another man's truthfulness by your own, from being imposed upon."

    Our Mutual Friend by Charles Dickens

    (a) development (b) resistance (c) credibility
    (d) deserving nature (e) tendency to believe

7. "Besides, D'Artagnan from her own admission knew Milady <u>culpable</u> of treachery in matters more important, and could entertain no respect for her."

    The Three Musketeers by Alexandre Dumas

    (a) believable (b) guilty (c) gullible (d) responsible
    (e) trustworthy

8. "He nodded gravely, and added with awful emphasis – 'I thought it <u>incumbent</u> upon me to do so.'"

    The Tenant of Wildfell Hall by Anne Bronte

    (a) obligatory (b) deserving (c) lying down (d) guilty (e) greedy

9. "After a <u>cursory</u> examination of the stateroom he wandered out into the cabin."

    Jerry of the Islands by Jack London

    (a) pithy (b) sacred (c) superficial (d) agreeable (e) limiting

10. "We are such <u>docile</u> creatures, normally, that it takes a virus to jolt us out of life's routine."

    The Cold by E.B. White

    (a) obedient (b) instructive (c) divine (d) creative (e) intuitive

11. "Samson embraced him, and entreated him to let him hear of his good or evil fortunes, so that he might rejoice over the former or <u>condole</u> with him over the latter, as the laws of friendship required."

    Don Quixote by Miguel Cervantes

    (a) celebrate (b) express sorrow (c) despair (d) fight (e) depart

12. "He was never more sinister than when he was most polite, which is probably the truest test of breeding; and the elegance of his <u>diction</u>, even when he was swearing, no less than the distinction of his demeanour, showed him one of a different cast from his crew."

    The Adventures of Peter Pan by James Matthew Barrie

(a) blessing   (b) authority   (c) simple song   (d) enunciation   (e) rule

13. "Before Charles, King of France, passed into Italy, this country was under the dominion of the Pope, the Venetians, the King of Naples, the Duke of Milan, and the Florentines."

    The Prince by Nicolo Machiavelli

    (a) colony   (b) residence   (c) sovereignty   (d) forbearance
    (e) military

14. "When the verdict was called for, the Jury declined, As the word was so puzzling to spell; but they ventured to hope that the Snark wouldn't mind, Undertaking that duty as well."

    The Hunting of the Snark by Lewis Carroll

    (a) saying farewell   (b) expressing sympathy   (c) relating to home
    (d) influencing power   (e) decision of a jury

15. "It was his boast that, in his younger days, nothing could hurt or daunt him; but he had 'lived too fast,' and injured his constitution by his excesses."

    Astoria by Washington Irving

    (a) fear   (b) determine   (c) dismay   (d) defeat   (e) control

16. "Nor did he see the dorsal fin break surface and approach him from the rear."

    Jerry of the Islands by Jack London

    (a) dormant   (b) on the back   (c) lowest   (d) frontal   (e) self-centered

17. "The writer praises that class of pleasure vessels, and I am willing to endorse his words, as any man who loves every craft afloat would be ready to do."

    The Mirror of the Sea by Joseph Conrad

    (a) approve   (b) ridicule   (c) reason   (d) declare   (e) intimidate

18. "I saw myself, too, from the dramatic standpoint, and I was pleased with my role of the trusted friend bringing back the errant husband to his forgiving wife."

    Moon and Sixpence by W. Somerset Maugham

    (a) wondering   (b) careless   (c) wandering   (d) mistaken
    (e) equal

19. "She traversed the immense viaduct, whose arches span untroubled meadows and the dreamy flow of Tewin Water."

Howards End by E. M. Forster

(a) deviation   (b) bridge   (c) water   (d) valley   (e) arch

20. "When I overtook them and stopped to say a word, I found them affable and confiding."

My Antonia by Willa Cather

(a) mistaken   (b) failing   (c) passionate   (d) friendly   (e) misleading

21. "There are five dangerous faults which may affect a general …."

The Art of War by Tzu Sun

(a) result in   (b) comply   (c) influence   (d) copy   (e) behave like

22. "It was an apparition from that hidden life which lies, like a dark by-street, behind the goodly ornamented facade that meets the sunlight and the gaze of respectable admirers."

Silas Marner by George Eliot

(a) antique enclosure   (b) front   (c) open space   (d) window view
(e) complex issue

23. "I was glad to get a facsimile of the letter written by this fine old German Robin Hood, though I was not able to read it."

A Tramp Abroad by Mark Twain

(a) inanimate object   (b) expression   (c) prose literature   (d) complexities
(e) copy

24. "He had a little round picture of the identical gray horse, caparisoned with the identical pillion, before which he used to do a sort of fetish worship, and abuse turnpike-roads and carriages.

Tom Brown's Schooldays by Thomas Hughes

(a) mistaken belief   (b) an error   (c) good natured   (d) idol
(e) passionate

25. "But if he should give them notice at Lady Day, Arthur and I must move heaven and earth to mollify him.

Adam Bede by George Eliot

(a) mislead   (b) fail   (c) appease   (d) alter   (e) correct

Lesson XV
fer/lat, festus, fid, fin

FER, LAT	*FESTUS*	*FID*	*FIN*
to bring; to bear	festive	belief; faith	end; limit

*confer, conifer, defer, dilatory, elation,
fertile, infer, refer, transfer, translate, festoon,
confidence, fidelity, infidel, affinity, confine, define, definitive, finite*

Word Definitions

confer
v. to grant a title, degree, benefit, or right
"Only the king or queen may confer knighthood on a deserving subject."
conferre to bring together, to gather: *con-* together + *ferre* to bring, to carry

conifer
n. a tree bearing cones with evergreen needle-like or scale-like leaves
"Pines, firs, and other conifers release seeds from layered cones."
conifer cone-bearing: *conus* cone + *ferre* to bring, to carry

defer
v. to put off for a later time, postpone; yield to
"I deferred writing my essay until the night before it was due."
differre to defer: *dis-* apart + *ferre* to bring, to carry

dilatory
adj. slow to act; intended to cause delay; tardy
"I was inexcusably dilatory in writing my Christmas thank-you notes; I didn't send them until May."
differre to defer: *dis-* apart + *latum* brought, carried (past participle of the verb *ferre*)

elation
n. great happiness and exhilaration
"The fans were filled with elation after their team scored the winning touchdown in the last second"
efferre to carry out, to raise: *ex-* away + *latum* brought, carried (past participle of the verb *ferre*)

fertile adj. producing or capable of producing abundant growth (vegetation)
"The inner city proved fertile ground for the gangs."
fertility (n.)
ferre to bring, to carry

infer v. to deduce from evidence and reasoning rather than from explicit statements
"Do I correctly infer that you are against abortion?"
inference (n.)
inferre to bring in, bring about: *in-* in + *ferre* to bring, to carry

refer v. to mention or allude to
"Refer to a dictionary to discover the meanings of unfamiliar words."
reference (n.)
referre to carry back: *re-* back, again + *ferre* to bring, to carry

transfer v. to move from one place to another; to move to another department
"Stevedores transfer cargo from ships to receiving docks, and vice versa."
transference (n.)
transferre to transfer or translate: *trans-* across + *ferre* to bring, to carry

translate v. to express in another language; to express equivalence in different terms
"One-hundred Euros translates to approximately $130."
translation (n.)
transferre to transfer or translate: *trans-* across + *latum* brought, carried (past participle of the verb *ferre*)

festive adj. relating to a feast day or festival; gay and celebratory
"His 90th birthday was very festive, even though his health was failing."
festival (n.)
festus festive; feast day

festoon n. an ornamental chain or garland of flowers, leaves, or ribbons hung in a curve
v. to decorate with a garland of flowers
"The platform at the nominating convention was festooned with flags."
festus festive; feast day

confidence n. trust or faith in a person or thing; a secret
"By revealing my friend's secret, I violated a confidence."
confinis boundary, border: *con-* together + *finis* end, limit

fidelity n. loyalty to a person, cause, or belief; resemblance to reality
"Early stereo record players were known as 'hi-fis' for their high degree of fidelity in reproducing the original musical performance."
fides faith

infidel n. a person who has no religion or who does not believe in the dominant or majority religion
"To a Muslim, anyone of a different dogma or religion is an infidel."
infidelis: in- not + *fidelis* faithful

LESSON XV FER/LAT, FESTUS, FID, FIN

affinity n. a spontaneous or natural liking or sympathy; a talent or leaning
"His affinity for animals made him an excellent veterinary technician."
affinis neighboring; related (inside the family): *ad-* toward + *finis* limit, boundary

confine v. to keep or restrict someone or something within certain limits (of space, scope, or time)
n. (used in plural) bounds or limits
"I don't care what you think: Confine your opinion to yourself."
confinis border, boundary: *con-* together + *finis* end, limit

define v. to state or describe exactly the nature, scope, or meaning of
"In Expressionist painting, objects are often ill-defined."
definition (n.)
definire to define, to determine: *de-* of, concerning + *finire* to limit, to finish

definitive adj. finished; done decisively and with authority
"Gibbon wrote a voluminous and definitive account of the Roman Empire's fall."
definire to define, to determine: *de-* of, concerning + *finire* to limit, to finish

finite adj. limited in size or extent
"Though it is boundless, the universe contains a finite amount of matter."
finire to limit, to finish

Exercise A

Fill in the blanks in the sentences below with the correct form of a word in the scroll above.

1. She _____ her house and most of her assets into her children's names, so that when she needed to go into a nursing home, she would qualify for government assistance.

2. Nancy Kerrigan, like many competitive figure skaters, displayed an _____ for the sport at a young age.

3. Every time Tom Brady begins to doubt himself, he rubs his Super Bowl ring and remembers the _____ he felt after winning the "big" game.

4. The librarian offered to _____ George to the antiquarian specialist, who could help him with his research.

5. Although Sean had taken three years of French, he was unable to _____ for his parents when they visited Paris because he was unaccustomed to the local accent and rapidity of speech.

6. A strong leader knows when to _____ to someone who has more knowledge.

7. The district attorney feared the defendant would be released unless she could quickly gather _____ evidence of his guilt.

8. His _____ driving habits caused him to be late.

9. When Harriet saw Steve holding hands with Miranda, she _____ that the two were dating.

10. At one time, the Pope was the most powerful man in the world; any leader who disobeyed him was labeled an _____ and removed from power.

11. He _____ a great honor on her when he chose her as his running-mate.

12. The number of human beings that the Earth can support is _____, although scientists do not agree on an exact figure.

13. A _____ of flowers decorated the sides of the garden club's parade float.

14. When Bruce contracted whooping cough, the school nurse decided that it would be best to _____ him to his home until he was fully recovered.

15. I had hoped their wedding would be a very _____ occasion, but they preferred a small, quiet ceremony with little fuss.

16. As Andrew struck out the first batters in his first Little League game, his _____ grew.

17. A successful marriage must have a strong foundation of good communication and mutual _____.

18. He couldn't _____ exactly what made her attractive, as no particular feature stood out.

19. Unlike deciduous trees, _____ remain green in winter.

20. The _____ valley of the Nile produces bountiful harvests.

LESSON XV FER/LAT, FESTUS, FID, FIN

Exercise B

Match the word with the letter of its definition.

1. ___ affinity
2. ___ confer
3. ___ confidence
4. ___ confine
5. ___ conifer
6. ___ defer
7. ___ define
8. ___ definitive
9. ___ dilatory
10. ___ festive
11. ___ fertile
12. ___ festoon
13. ___ fidelity
14. ___ finite
15. ___ elation
16. ___ infer
17. ___ infidel
18. ___ refer
19. ___ transfer
20. ___ translate

a) to express in another language
b) a person who does not believe in a particular religion; a heretic
c) tending to delay or put off things; not prompt
d) to make a logical assumption from inconclusive information
e) loyalty, faithfulness
f) to give or to bestow upon
g) a string of flowers or ribbons draped from two points
h) to keep within certain limits
i) to describe exactly
j) conclusive; completely authoritative
k) to submit to (the preference or knowledge of) another
l) a natural liking or preference
m) capable of supporting abundant growth
n) faith in oneself
o) having a limit
p) intense feeling of joy
q) to move (something) from one place to another
r) gay and celebratory
s) a cone-bearing tree
t) to mention or allude to

Exercise C

Solve the crossword puzzle.

Across
1 A person who has no religion or who does not believe in the dominant or majority religion **6** Producing or capable of producing abundant growth (vegetation) **7** To mention or allude to **8** A tree bearing cones with evergreen needle-like or scale-like leaves **9** To keep or restrict someone or something within certain limits; bounds or limits **11** Loyalty to a person, cause, or belief; resemblance to reality **14** To put off for a later time, postpone; yield to **17** To move from one place to another; to move to another department **18** To express in another language; to express equivalence in different terms **19** To grant a title, degree, benefit, or right **20** Trust or faith in a person or thing; a secret

Down
2 Limited in size or extent **3** To state or describe exactly the nature, scope, or meaning of **4** A spontaneous or natural liking or sympathy; a talent or leaning **5** Relating to a feast day or festival; gay and celebratory **10** To deduce from evidence and reasoning rather than from explicit statements **12** Finished; done decisively and with authority **13** An ornamental chain or garland of flowers, leaves, or ribbons hung in a curve; to decorate with a garland of flowers **15** Slow to act; intended to cause delay; tardy **16** Great happiness and exhilaration

Lesson XVI
fingo/figuro, firm, flect/flex, flor, flu

FINGO, FIGURO
to shape

FIRM
strong

FLECT, FLEX
to bend

FLOR
flower

FLU
to flow

*configuration, figurative, affirm, confirm, infirm, infirmary,
deflect, genuflect, inflection, flora, floral, florid,
affluent, confluent, effluent, fluctuate, fluent, fluid, flux, influx*

Word Definitions

configuration **n.** an arrangement of parts or elements in a particular form or figure
"A baseball infield has a diamond-shaped <u>configuration</u>."
configure (v.)
configurare to shape after a pattern: *con-* together + *figurare* to shape

figurative **adj.** departing from a literal use of words; metaphorical
"To be 'in hot water' is a <u>figurative</u> expression meaning to be in trouble."
fingere to form, contrive, shape

affirm **v.** to state emphatically or publicly; to support the validity of
"The First Amendment <u>affirms</u> a citizen's right to free speech."
affirmative (adj.)
affirmare to affirm, to assert: *ad-* to + *firmus* strong

confirm **v.** to establish the truth or correctness of
"The timely arrival of the comet <u>confirmed</u> Halley's prediction from years earlier."
confirmation (n.)
confirmare to strength, to secure: *con-* together + *firmare* to strengthen

infirm	**adj.** not physically strong, especially because of age "A veterans' hospital houses infirm soldiers." *infirmus* weak, sick: *in-* not + *firmus* firm, strong
infirmary	**n.** a place within a larger institution for the care of those who are ill or injured; a hospital "The outbreak of mononucleosis on campus filled the beds of the college infirmary." *infirmus* weak, sick: *in-* not + *firmus* firm, strong
deflect	**v.** to deviate or cause to deviate from a straight course "The bullet was deflected by the wall and hit a bystander." *deflection (n.)* *deflectere* to deflect: *de-* from + *flectere* to bend
genuflect	**v.** to lower one's body briefly by bending one knee to the ground in worship or as a sign of respect "He always genuflects before entering the family pew at St. John's." *genuflection (n.)* *genuflectere* to kneel down: *genu* knee + *flectere* to bend
inflection	**n.** a change in the form of a word to express a grammatical function or attribute; specific pronunciation of a word or syllable "One can tell the regional origins of a speaker based on his inflection." *inflectere* to bend, to change *in-* into + *flectere* to bend
flora	**n.** the plants of a particular region, habitat, or geological period (compare with fauna) "Antibiotics kill intestinal flora, often disrupting digestion by eliminating both beneficial and harmful bacteria." *flos, floris* flower
floral	**adj.** relating to or decorated with flowers "The tables were decorated with colorful floral arrangements." *flos, floris* flower
florid	**adj.** having a red or flushed complexion; flowery; ornate "Ancient orators sometimes used highly contrived and florid language." *flos, floris* flower
affluent	**adj.** wealthy; (of water) flowing freely or copiously "Affluent people often flaunt their wealth by driving expensive cars." *affluence (n.)* *affluere* flow toward, flow freely: *af-* toward + *fluere* to flow
confluent	**adj.** flowing together; blended into one **n.** one of two or more confluent streams; a tributary "The two rivers become confluent just north of the city." *confluence (n.)* *confluere* to flow together: *con-* together + *fluere* to flow

LESSON XVI FINGO/FIGURO, FIRM, FLECT/FLEX, FLOR, FLU

effluent n. the liquid waste or sewage discharged into a river or the sea
"The chemical company was fined for discharging <u>effluent</u> into the river."
effluere to flow out: *ex-* out + *fluere* to flow

fluctuate v. to rise and fall irregularly in number or amount; to waver
"Stock prices may <u>fluctuate</u> wildly when there's overall economic uncertainty."
fluctuation (n.)
fluctuare to undulate, to rise in waves < *fluere* to flow

fluent adj. speaking or writing easily and accurately, especially in a foreign language
"After living in Paris for a decade, she spoke <u>fluent</u> French."
fluere to flow

fluid n. a substance that has no fixed shape and yields easily to external pressure; a liquid or gas
adj. able to flow easily; not settled or stable
"The game is still <u>fluid</u>; either side could win."
fluidity (n.)
fluere to flow

flux n. the action or process of flowing; continuous change
"His mood is always in <u>flux</u>, depending on whether he remembers to take his medication on time."
fluere to flow

influx n. an arrival or entry of large numbers of people or things
"The United States has seen a great influx of illegal immigrants from Mexico in recent decades, as the Mexican economy has lagged."
influere to flow in: *in-* into + *fluere* to flow

Exercise A

Fill in the blanks in the sentences below with the correct form of a word in the scroll above.

1. My father became so weak he could no longer care for himself, and had to enter a home for aging and _____ veterans.

2. The _____ of families with children has strained the town's school system.

3. Daniel's biting wit and clever use of _____ language caught the attention of Mr. Meade, his ninth-grade English teacher.

4. Serge's heart palpitations caused his pulse to _____.

107

5. The linebacker tried to _____ Tom Brady's pass, but Troy Brown recovered to catch the ball anyway.

6. Steven King's _____ writing style pulls the reader into the story.

7. Astrologers believe that the _____ of the planets at a person's birth determines his or her unique personality.

8. Her comical _____ belied the sad facts of her story.

9. The wedding planner designed an intricate _____ arrangement for the head table.

10. The _____ from the city's homes and businesses flowed into Boston Harbor for centuries, making it one of the most polluted bodies of water in the world.

11. Jay-Z planned to _____ rumors of his retirement during an interview on MTV.

12. It was a hot, humid summer evening, and the young woman's pink cheeks looked even more _____ in the reddish light of the setting sun.

13. Her thoughts about which job to accept were in a state of _____.

14. The _____ and fauna of Burma were documented in a National Geographic film.

15. The dancer's movements were _____ and graceful, even when she was doing something as ordinary as grocery shopping.

16. His speech _____ my belief in the power of love to work miracles.

17. The Army _____ was equipped to treat injured soldiers and Iraqi civilians alike.

18. It was amazing to see 30,000 people _____ simultaneously when the Pope entered the plaza.

19. The Little River is a _____ of the Merrimack River.

20. The more _____ couples were happy to sponsor the dance, paying for the entertainment as well as the refreshments.

Exercise B

Match the word with the letter of its definition.

1. ___ affirm
2. ___ affluent
3. ___ configuration
4. ___ confirm
5. ___ confluent
6. ___ deflect
7. ___ effluent
8. ___ figurative
9. ___ flora
10. ___ floral
11. ___ florid
12. ___ fluctuate
13. ___ fluent
14. ___ fluid
15. ___ flux
16. ___ genuflect
17. ___ infirmary
18. ___ infirm
19. ___ inflection
20. ___ influx

a) pertaining to flowers
b) to vary
c) using figures of speech; metaphorical
d) continuous change
e) plants
f) expressed readily and effortlessly
g) to cause to change direction; to redirect
h) to establish the truth of
i) an arrival of many
j) a change in tone or pitch of voice
k) a hospital within a larger institution
l) an ordering or arrangement
m) flushed with rosy color
n) flowing together as one
o) wealthy
p) moving readily and smoothly
q) to state emphatically or publicly
r) to go down on one knee to show worship or respect
s) liquid waste discharged into a body of water
t) not physically strong

Exercise C

Solve the crossword puzzle:

Across
3. moving readily and smoothly
6. an ordering or agreement
8. flushed with rosy color
12. liquid waste discharged into a body of water
14. plants
16. not physically strong
17. an arrival of many
19. to establish the truth of

Down
1. wealthy
2. pertaining to flowers
4. to cause to change direction; to redirect
5. using figures of speech; metaphorical
7. to go down on one knee to show worship or respect
9. a hospital with a larger institution
10. expressed readily and effortlessly
11. flowing together as one
13. a change in tone or pitch of voice
15. to state emphatically or publicly
18. continuous change
20. to vary

Lesson XVII
fort-, fors/fort, forum, frag/fract, frater, frons, fug

FORT-	**FORS, FORT-**	**FORUM**	**FRAG, FRACT**
strong	luck; chance	a place outdoors	to break

FRATER	**FRONS**	**FUG-**
brother	front	flee

---

fortuitous, fortunate, fortify, fortitude, forensic, forum, fracture, fragment, fragile, frail, infraction, infringe, refractory, fraternal, fraternize, fratricide, affront, confront, fugitive, refuge

---

Word Definitions

fortuitous **adj.** happening by chance rather than by intention; lucky
"My finding a $20 bill on the ground was <u>fortuitous.</u>"
fortuity (n.)
fors, fortis luck, chance

fortunate **adj.** favored by or involving good luck
"Those still in perfect health in their eighties are <u>fortunate</u> indeed."
fortune (n.)
fors, fortis luck, chance

fortify **v.** to provide with defenses against attack; to strengthen
"Many breakfast cereals are <u>fortified</u> with vitamins to increase their nutritional value."
fortification (n.)
fortifacere to make strong < *forte, fortis* strong

fortitude **n.** mental or emotional strength in facing adversity
"She showed great <u>fortitude</u> in caring for her dying mother at home."
forte, fortis strong

forensic	**adj.** denoting scientific methods and evidence in crimes; having to do with courts of law or formal debate "Those with great <u>forensic</u> skill are admired in Congress, where they have endless opportunities for debate." *forum* out of doors (in open court)
forum	**n.** a meeting place or medium for an exchange of views "PTA meetings constitute a <u>forum</u> for parents to air grievances and work with teachers to improve the school's performance." *forum* out of doors
fracture	**n.** a crack or break, especially in a bone **v.** to crack or break "The roar of cannons <u>fractured</u> the silence of the countryside." *frangere* to break
fragment	**n.** a small part broken off or detached "The explosion sent scores of glass <u>fragments</u> flying through the air." *frangere* to break
fragile	**adj.** easily broken or damaged "The starving refugees looked terribly <u>fragile</u>." *frangere* to break
frail	**adj.** weak and delicate "The elderly woman was so <u>frail</u> her children feared that if she fell she would shatter her hip." *frailty (n.)* *frangere* to break
infraction	**n.** a violation or breaking of a law or agreement "Parking in a handicapped space without a sticker is an <u>infraction</u> carrying a $200 fine." *infringere* to break off, to weaken: *in-* into + *frangere* to break
infringe	**v.** to break a law, agreement, etc.; to encroach on a right, privilege, or territory "The editor cut her work so often that the columnist felt it <u>infringed</u> on her contract, which stated she was free to express her political opinions." *infringement (n.)* *infringere* to break off, to weaken: *in-* into + *frangere* to break
refractory	**adj.** stubborn or unmanageable; resisting ordinary methods or treatment "Their son's behavior became so <u>refractory</u> they sought the help of a family systems therapist." *refractus* to break up (past participle of the verb *refrangere*): *re-* back, again + *frangere* to break
fraternal	**adj.** of or like a brother(s) "A club that admits males only is a <u>fraternal</u> organization." *fraternity (n.)* *frater* brother

LESSON XVII FORT-, FORS/FORT, FORUM, FRAG/FRACT, FRATER, FRONS, FUG

fraternize	**v.** to be on friendly terms with; to socialize with "French women who <u>fraternized</u> with Nazi soldiers were ostracized or punished after the war." *frater* brother
fratricide	**n.** the killing of one's brother or sister "Cain committed the first <u>fratricide</u> when he murdered his brother, Abel." *frater* brother
affront	**n.** an action or remark that causes outrage or offense **v.** to offend the modesty or values of "Burning the American flag is considered an <u>affront</u> to all patriots." *ad frontem* to the face of: *ad-* to, toward + *frontem* face, front
confront	**v.** to stand or meet face to face with hostile intent or anger "A psychiatrist may help you to <u>confront</u> long-repressed emotions." *confrontation* (n.) *confrontare* to confront: *con-* with, together + *frons, front-* face
fugitive	**n.** a person who has escaped from captivity or is in hiding **adj.** quick to disappear; fleeting "<u>Fugitive</u> shadows passed rapidly across the darkening sky." *fugere* to flee
refuge	**n.** a place or state of safety from danger or trouble "When a thunderstorm broke out, Dido and Aeneas took <u>refuge</u> in a cave." *refugium* refuge: *re-* back + *fugere* to flee

Exercise A

Fill in the blanks in the sentences below with the correct form of a word in the scroll above.

1. The _____ infection resisted treatment with several common antibiotics.

2. When the wind blew through the open window, the _____ vase fell off the shelf and shattered.

3. The philosopher used his college classroom as a _____ to test many of his controversial ideas before subjecting them to the harsher criticism of his peers.

4. His drunken behavior at the funeral was an _____ to the grieving family.

5. Benedict Arnold, an American general, is infamous for _____ with the British during the Revolutionary War.

6. While scaling Mount Everest, one of the climbers _____ his big toe.

7. Despite the fact that shoplifting expensive goods is a felony, the judge in Winona Ryder's case treated it as a minor _____.

8. The _____ hid in a Dumpster for three days, surviving on leftovers in the garbage, until a police dog discovered him.

9. It's _____ that I ran into you here, as I was just about to call you and see if you could babysit Saturday night.

10. The newborn kittens were so _____ that June feared their mother would crush them when she lay down.

11. We were all _____ to graduate before the school lowered its standards and a degree became meaningless.

12. Anne Frank's family found _____ in the attic of the house of a family friend during the German occupation of Holland.

13. Using modern _____ tools, investigators were able to lift fingerprints from the crime scene and compare them with those of the suspect.

14. The boys had a _____ connection; they regarded each other as members of an extended family.

15. Dogs are very territorial and can react angrily when strangers or other animals _____ on their turf.

16. Archaeologists spend much of their time trying to piece together _____ of pottery to determine a vessel's shape and use.

17. He _____ himself with a glass of whiskey before meeting his future in-laws.

18. The drunken teenager _____ the police officer, and ended up getting charged with resisting arrest.

19. _____ is very unusual, but court battles between siblings – especially those in a family business – are more common.

20. Both of them hoped they would have the _____ to withstand both the questioning during the trial and the media circus afterwards.

LESSON XVII FORT-, FORS/FORT, FORUM, FRAG/FRACT, FRATER, FRONS, FUG

Exercise B

Match the word with the letter of its definition.

1. ___ affront
2. ___ confront
3. ___ fortuitous
4. ___ fortunate
5. ___ fortify
6. ___ forensic
7. ___ fortitude
8. ___ forum
9. ___ fraternal
10. ___ fraternize
11. ___ fracture
12. ___ fragile
13. ___ fragment
14. ___ frail
15. ___ fratricide
16. ___ fugitive
17. ___ infraction
18. ___ infringe
19. ___ refractory
20. ___ refuge

a) pertaining to the acquisition of evidence for court
b) to strengthen to defend against attack
c) weak; in poor health
d) to face in anger or with hostility
e) happening by accident or chance
f) a location protected from enemies; a shelter
g) easily breakable
h) a place or medium for discussion
i) pertaining to or characteristic of brothers
j) the breaking of a rule, law, agreement, etc.
k) a broken piece of a whole
l) one who flees from the law
m) to break, especially a bone
n) ability to endure suffering
o) difficult or stubborn
p) to be on friendly terms
q) the killing of one's brother or sister
r) an offense (against someone)
s) to encroach on a right or territory
t) favored by or involving good luck

Exercise C

Solve the crossword puzzle.

Across
2. Favored by or involving good luck. 7. Weak, delicate (of health). 10. A crack or break. 11. The killing of one's brother. 12. A meeting or medium for an exchange of views. 13. An action or remark that causes outrage or offense. 16. Stubborn or unmanageable; resistant to normal treatment. 18. Denoting the application of scientific methods to investigation of evidence for court; involving debate skills.

Down
1. Brotherly. 2. A small part, broken off. 3. A violation of a law or an agreement. 4. To provide with defenses against attack. 5. One who has escaped from captivity or is in hiding from the law. 6. Easily broken or damaged. 7. Happening by chance. 8. To violate a law or contract; to encroach on a right. 9. A place of safety. 14. To socialize with. 15. Courage in facing adversity. 17. To face with hostile intent.

Lesson XVIII
fus, gargo, gen/genere

FUS-	*GARGO*	*GEN, GENERE*
to pour	throat	class, kind

diffuse, effusive, fusion, profuse, transfuse, gorge, regurgitate, congenital, engender, generate, generous, genre, genteel, gentile, gentry, genuine, genus, ingenuous, progenitor, regenerate

Word Definitions

diffuse
v. to spread over a wide area
adj. spread out over a wide area; lacking clarity
"The crop duster dropped the herbicide, which <u>diffused</u> in a cloud over the fields."
diffusus spread out, scattered: *de-* down, from + *fusus* poured (past participle of the verb *fundere* to pour)

effusive
adj. expressing gratitude, pleasure, or approval in an unrestrained manner
"My <u>effusive</u> aunt hugged those near her and blew air kisses to everyone else."
effusus vast, extravagant: *ex-* out + *fusus* poured

fusion
n. the process or result of joining together into a unit; a reaction in which light atomic nuclei meld to form a heavier nucleus
"The <u>fusion</u> of nickel and chromium makes Nichrome coils."
fusus poured < *fundere* to pour, to melt (metal)

profuse
adj. plentiful; abundant
"The tardy guest made <u>profuse</u> apologies, repeating 'I'm sorry' two dozen times."
profusus excessive, lavish: *pro-* forth + *fusus* poured

transfuse
v. to transfer (blood or blood components); to permeate or infuse with something
"Stored blood is <u>transfused</u> into accident victims who've bled heavily."
transfusus poured from one container to another: *trans-* across + *fusus* poured

gorge	**n.** a steep, narrow valley or ravine **v.** to eat a large amount greedily "The ravenous lions <u>gorged</u> themselves on the dead zebra." *gorges* throat
regurgitate	**v.** to bring undigested food up from the stomach; to repeat (something) without analyzing or comprehending it "The pupil could <u>regurgitate</u> the rules, but couldn't apply them." *regurgitation (n.)* *regurgitare* to vomit, regurgitate: *re-* again + *gorges* throat
congenital	**adj.** present from birth "Czar Nicholas' son was born with hemophilia, a <u>congenital</u> blood disease." *congenitus* existing from birth; arising together: *con-* together + *gignere* to be born, to give birth
engender	**v.** to give rise to "The coming of winter and reduced sunlight <u>engender</u> depression in some people." *ingenerare* to implant: *en-* in + *generare* to beget, to father
generate	**v.** to cause; to produce "The shouting match over the controversial bill <u>generated</u> more heat than light." *generation (n.)* *generare* to beget, to father
generous	**adj.** freely giving more of something than is necessary or expected "The teacher was <u>generous</u> with praise and encouragement." *generosity (n.)* *generosus* noble, magnanimous
genre	**n.** a style or category of art or literature "Poetry, drama, and novels represent different literary <u>genres</u>." *genere* to bring forth, to bear < *genus* birth, origin, family, type
genteel	**adj.** exaggeratedly or affectedly polite and refined; well-mannered "You need never be nervous about taking <u>genteel</u> people to high-society parties." *gentilis* of a family or nation, of the same clan < *gens, gent-* family, race
gentile	**adj.** not Jewish; not belonging to one's own religious community "Paul offended some Jews by preaching to <u>gentiles</u> as well." *gentilis* of a family or nation, of the same clan < *gens, gent-* tribe, people
gentry	**n.** people of good social position; the class just below the nobility "In Victorian England, the <u>gentry</u>'s country pastime was fox hunting." *gentilis* of a family or nation, of the same clan < *gens, gent-* tribe, people

LESSON XVIII FUS, GARGO, GEN/GENERE

genuine adj. truly what it is said to be; authentic, sincere, honest
"The derringer was the genuine article, not a copy."
genus birth, descent, type

genus n. a principal taxonomic category that ranks above species and below family
"Humans are biologically classified as the species *sapiens* and genus *homo*."
genus birth, descent, type

ingenuous adj. innocent and unsuspecting; candid
"Her unflattering question was so ingenuous he could not take offense."
ingenuus generous, frank

progenitor n. an ancestor or parent
"George H.W. Bush was the progenitor of George W. Bush."
progignere to beget, produce: *pro-* forward + *gignere* to beget

regenerate v. (of a living organism) to regrow a limb or tissue; to bring new and more vigorous life to (an area or institution)
"The $10 million contribution regenerated the ailing museum."
regeneration (n.)
regenerare to create again: *re-* again + *generare* to be born, to give birth

Exercise A

Fill in the blanks in the sentences below with the correct form of a word in the scroll above.

1. The Windows operating system was the _____ of Microsoft Vista.

2. Being dependent on the charity of others can _____ resentment.

3. Both Jewish and _____ holidays are celebrated in December.

4. Because of a _____ defect, the infant required surgery.

5. At first she found it hard to credit David's innocent attitude, but she later concluded that he was truly naïve and _____.

6. The Iron Chef's _____ of French cooking techniques with Asian ingredients and presentation created exciting and delicious new dishes.

7. The huge _____ known as the Grand Canyon was created by a combination of seismic activity and erosion by the Colorado River.

8. She was _____ with delight when he accepted her proposal.

9. Many of today's teen idols wear _____ amounts of makeup on stage.

10. The _____ of science fiction is constantly evolving with developments in science and technology.

11. We may consider wealthy indulgence to be a modern dilemma, but the old English _____ spent their days attending theatrical performances and playing croquet while peasants struggled and city dwellers went to debtors' prisons.

12. Her parents are always very _____ with gifts for the holidays.

13. One classic example of chaos theory is that a drop of blue dye put into a beaker of water will never _____ through the liquid in the same pattern twice.

14. Although John McCain has voiced his support for President Bush, many experts believe his endorsement is not _____.

15. Nuclear plants can _____ enough electricity to power a sizeable city.

16. Her manner was so _____ and refined that you'd never have guessed she grew up in a rough part of town.

17. The coach's _____ praise of the star player irritated the other players.

18. Starfish have the ability to _____ their limbs if they are torn, cut, or bitten off by predators.

19. On late night television, one can witness a man swallow a closed lock and, separately, a key, then _____ the opened lock with the key in it.

20. Scientific names, comprised of an organism's _____ and species, are typically too long and difficult to pronounce and spell for everyday use.

Exercise B

Match the word with the letter of its definition.

1. ___ congenital
2. ___ diffuse
3. ___ effusive
4. ___ fusion
5. ___ engender
6. ___ generate
7. ___ generous
8. ___ genre
9. ___ genteel
10. ___ gentile
11. ___ gentry
12. ___ genuine
13. ___ genus
14. ___ gorge
15. ___ ingenuous
16. ___ profuse
17. ___ progenitor
18. ___ regenerate
19. ___ regurgitate
20. ___ transfuse
21. ___ diffusion

a) to vomit; to repeat without understanding
b) innocent and naive
c) to create; to propagate
d) an originator of a line of descent
e) the result or process of fusing
f) expressing excessive gratitude or pleasure
g) polite, well mannered
h) to grow again
i) to transfer, to permeate
j) a wealthy or high-born class of people
k) to give rise to; to stimulate
l) freely giving more of something than needed or sought
m) a narrow ravine
n) to spread over a wide area
o) a type or category (of literature or art)
p) present from birth
q) plentiful
r) authentic, real
s) a category of organisms
t) a person who is not Jewish
u) the action of spreading (something) through a medium

Exercise C

Solve the crossword puzzle

Across
2. to vomit; to repeat without understanding
4. a type or category (of literature or art)
5. to transfer, to permeate
8. a wealthy or high-born class of people
9. a category of organisms
11. a person who is not Jewish
13. to give rise to; to stimulate
14. expressing excessive gratitude or sorrow
15. polite, well mannered
17. innocent and naive
18. to spread over a wide area
19. present from birth
20. an originator of a line of descent

Down
1. the action of spreading (something) through a medium
3. freely giving more of something than needed or sought
6. plentiful
7. authentic, real
9. to create; to propagate
10. the result or process of fusing
12. to grow again
16. a narrow ravine

Lesson XIX
glomus, grad/gress, grat, greg

GLOMUS	*GRAD, GRESS*	*GRAT*	*GREG*
ball	**go; step; advance**	**please; favor**	**flock, herd**

conglomerate, degrade, digress, gradient, gradual, graduate, ingredient, progress, regress, retrograde, transgress, congratulation, grateful, gratify, gratitude, aggregate, congregation, egregious, gregarious, segregation

Word Definitions

conglomerate   n. something made up of different things brought together; a business with several distinct subsidiaries
adj. made up of separate elements
v. to bring disparate elements together
"The business was a conglomerate of textbook publishing, educational testing, and teacher training divisions."
conglomeration (n.)
conglomerare to concentrate, gather into a compact mass: *con-* together + *glomus, glomeris* ball-shaped mass < *globus* ball

degrade   v. to cause to suffer a severe loss of dignity or respect; to demean; to cause to break down or deteriorate
"In winter, the road surface degrades from repeated freezes and thaws that cause cracks and potholes."
degradation (n.)
degradare to reduce in rank, degrade: *de-* down, from + *gradus* grade

digress   v. to go off on a tangent, or leave the main subject briefly, in speech or writing
"The president digressed from economic policy to mention his recent physical."

	digression (n.) *digredi* to depart; to divorce: *di-* aside + *gradi* to walk
gradient	**n.** the degree of slope of a road or railway; a slope or ramp "The Egyptian pyramids have a steep <u>gradient</u> from ground to apex." *gradus* step, position
gradual	**adj.** taking place in stages, or slowly, over an extended period "There has been a <u>gradual</u> decline in the number of patrons at our restaurant over the past three years." *gradus* step, position
graduate	**v.** to successfully complete a degree, course, or school; to mark with measurements **n.** a person who has been awarded an academic degree or high school diploma "An American yardstick is <u>graduated</u> by 1/16ths of an inch." *graduation (n.)* *graduare* to take a degree < *gradus* step, position
ingredient	**n.** any of the foods or substances that are combined to make a particular dish; a component or element "Inspiration, hard work, and a little luck are the basic <u>ingredients</u> of success." *ingredi* to enter: *in-* into + *gradi* to take steps, to advance
progress	**n.** forward or onward movement toward a destination; development toward a better, more complete, or more modern condition **v.** to move or develop toward a destination, goal, or better condition "Thomas Edison never <u>progressed</u> beyond grade school." *progression (n.)* *progredi* to come forth, make progress: *pro-* forward + *gradi* to take steps, to advance
regress	**v.** to return to a former state; to go backward **n.** the act of regressing "Venus at times appears to <u>regress</u>, or double back, in its orbit." *regression (n.)* *regredi* to go back, to return: *re-* again + *gradi* to take steps, to advance
retrograde	**adj.** directed or moving backwards; reverting to an earlier or inferior condition "When shifted into reverse, a car's motion can be made <u>retrograde</u>." *retro* backward + *gradus* step
transgress	**v.** to go beyond the limits set by (a moral, principle, standard, law, etc.); to overstep a boundary "By eating the forbidden fruit, Eve <u>transgressed</u> God's command." *transgression (n.)* *transgredi* to step across: *trans-* across + *gradi* to take steps, to advance

congratulation	**n.** praise or good wishes on a special occasion "By way of congratulation, Mr. Smith bought his son a car." *congratulatory (adj.), congratulate (v.)* *congratulari* to congratulate, share joy with: *con-* with + *gratulari* to show joy < *gratus* pleasing
grateful	**adj.** feeling or showing gratitude "A grateful child never minds writing thank-you notes for birthday gifts." *grate* pleasantly, thankfully < *gratus* pleasing, thankful
gratify	**v.** to give pleasure or satisfaction to; to indulge or satisfy a desire "The moviegoer gratified his hunger with a bucket of popcorn." *gratificari* to oblige or do as a favor: *gratus* pleasing + *facere* to make
gratitude	**n.** appreciation of kindness; thankfulness "The woman expressed gratitude to the firefighters who saved her kitten." *gratus* pleasing, thankful
aggregate	**n.** a whole formed by a collection of particulars; the total sum or amount **adj.** formed or calculated by the combination of many separate units or items **v.** to combine into a whole "His stocks, bonds, and real estate aggregate to a net worth greater than $1 million." *aggregation (n.)* *aggregare* to herd together: *ad-* toward + *grex, gregis* a flock
congregation	**n.** a gathering of people or things: a group of people assembled for religious worship "A congregation of dozens of crows blackened the crown of the tree." *congregate (v.)* *congregare* to collect (into a flock): *con-* together + *gregare* to gather
egregious	**adj.** outstandingly bad "Hitler is considered among the most egregious leaders in history." *egregius* standing out from the flock: *ex-* out + *grex, gregis* a flock
gregarious	**adj.** fond of company; sociable; living in herds "Sheep and cows are gregarious animals, while cats and spiders are solitary." *gregarius* belonging to the flock < *gregare* to gather (into a flock)
segregation	**n.** the act of separating and keeping apart; separation by race or religion *segregate (v.)* "The Constitution mandates the segregation of power into three branches." *segregare* to remove, to separate (from the flock) < *grex, gregis* a flock

Exercise A

Fill in the blanks in the sentences below with the correct form of a word in the scroll above.

1. Although Tiger Woods made four shots above par on Friday, his _____ score from all four rounds was 243, good enough for third place.

2. While some Episcopal _____ and ministers support the blessing of same-sex unions, others do not, which has caused a deep division within the church.

3. The dune rose at a gentle _____, formed by the same winds that limited its height.

4. The terraces the Incas carved into the mountainside formed a _____ staircase leading to the lofty peak.

5. He _____ his college-educated wife by refusing to let her work, humiliating her in front of others, and treating her like a servant.

6. Try as they might, the students could not get their teacher to _____ from his favorite topic, chemistry.

7. Billy _____ his parents by getting accepted to Princeton University, continuing the family legacy.

8. The most important _____ in steak au poivre is the steak.

9. Although Simon realized he had already _____ by entering the abandoned warehouse, his curiosity got the best of him and he pressed on.

10. _____ in the pre-civil rights era South was the legacy of slavery.

11. The elderly lady's face glowed with _____ when the Boy Scout offered to carry her groceries.

12. Scott's _____ nature eventually led him to a career in theater.

13. We parked on _____ without setting the emergency break and turning the wheels to the curb, and the car rolled down the hill.

14. She is the most _____ flirt I have ever met.

15. We made excellent _____ on our trip from San Francisco to Chicago, traveling more than 500 miles each day.

126

LESSON XIX GLOMUS, GRAD/GRESS, GRAT, GREG

16. As the giant snowball rolled downhill, it became a _____ of twigs, gravel, and abandoned mittens it picked up along the way.

17. The New England Patriots were thrilled to receive personal _____ from President Bush for winning the Super Bowl.

18. The autistic boy was doing very well in school, but he _____ after his family moved and he had to change schools, teachers, and special education aides.

19. The students were _____ for the unexpected snow day, but working parents were left scrambling for child care.

20. The day we _____ from high school was the happiest in our lives.

Exercise B

Match the word with the letter of its definition.

1. ___ aggregate
2. ___ conglomerate
3. ___ congratulation
4. ___ congregation
5. ___ degrade
6. ___ digress
7. ___ egregious
8. ___ gradient
9. ___ gradual
10. ___ graduate
11. ___ grateful
12. ___ gratify
13. ___ gratitude
14. ___ gregarious
15. ___ ingredient
16. ___ progress
17. ___ regress
18. ___ retrograde
19. ___ segregation
20. ___ transgress

a) taking place in slow stages
b) disparate parts combined into a whole
c) appreciation; thankfulness
d) separation (often by race or religion)
e) moving backward
f) a group of assembled people
g) approval of an achievement
h) outstandingly bad; horrible
i) the sum of smaller parts
j) to please or satisfy; to give pride to
k) to move forward or develop an improved condition
l) to successfully complete a degree or diploma
m) outgoing and fond of being around others
n) to go back or return to a previous state
o) to go beyond the limits of; to cross a boundary
p) a component or element
q) to decrease in rank or quality; to humiliate
r) feeling or showing gratitude
s) the slope (of a road or railway)
t) to stray from the main topic

Exercise C

Solve the crossword puzzle.

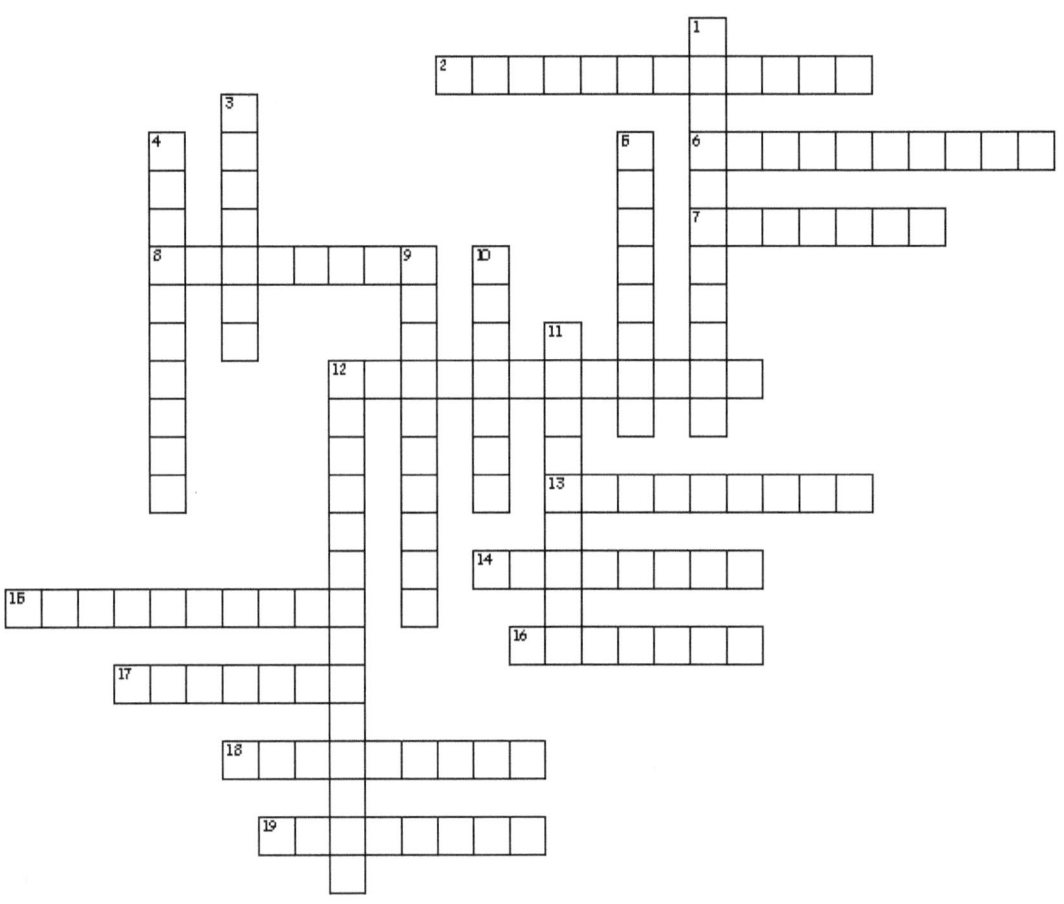

Across
2. Something consisting of different and distinct things grouped together. 6. Directed or moving backwards. 7. To give pleasure or satisfaction. 8. The slope (of a road or railway). 12. A gathering of people or things; members of a church. 13. Outstandingly bad. 14. Feeling or showing gratitude. 15. A component or element used to make something. 16. To return to a former state, go backward. 17. Taking place slowly over an extended period. 18. Thankfulness. 19. Movement toward a destination.

Down
1. The action of segregating or the state of being segregated. 3. To cause to suffer a severe loss of dignity or respect; to demean. 4. Outgoing and sociable. 5. To successfully complete an educational degree or course of study. 9. To go beyond the limits set. 10. To go off on a tangent. 11. To combine into a whole. 12. Praise or good wishes on a special occasion.

Lesson XX
her/hes, impleo, incendo, ira, iter/itiner, ire

HER, HES	***IMPLEO***	***INCENDO***	***IRE***
to stick	to fill	to set on fire	to to

IRA	***ITER, ITINER***
anger	journey, road

adhere, adhesion, adhesive, coherent, cohesion, incoherent, inherent, deplete, expletive, implement, replete, incendiary, incense, irascible, irate, circuit, circuitous, itinerant, itinerary, transit, transition, transitory

Word Definitions

adhere
v. to stick fast to
"Puritans <u>adhered</u> to a strict and demanding orthodoxy."
adhaerere to adhere: *ad-* to + *haerere* to stick

adhesion
n. the action or process of adhering or sticking to
"The <u>adhesion</u> of water-based paste breaks down in moist conditions."
adhaerere to adhere: *ad-* to + *haerere* to stick

adhesive
adj. sticky
n. glue
"The masking tape was not <u>adhesive</u> enough to hold up the poster."
adhaerere to adhere: *ad-* to + *haerere* to stick

coherent
adj. holding together to form a whole; logical and consistent
"John spoke eloquently at his mother's memorial service; I was impressed by his ability to remain <u>coherent</u> when he was so upset."
coherence (n.)
cohaerere to bind together: *co-* together + *haerere* to stick

cohesion	**n.** the action of forming a united whole (a sticking together) "The cohesion of the social group was threatened when one man fell in love with another's wife." *cohesive (adj.)* *cohaerere* to bind together: *co-* together + *haerere* to stick
incoherent	**adj.** incomprehensible or confusing "Awkward prose and multiple viewpoints made her essay incoherent." *incoherence (n.)* *in-* not, against + *cohaerere* to bind together
inherent	**adj.** existing in something as a permanent or essential attribute "Flowers have inherent beauty, because they are designed to attract the insects or animals they depend on for reproduction." *inhaerere* to cling to: *in-* in, upon + *haerere* to stick
deplete	**v.** to reduce the number or quantity of; to empty "After running four miles in the hot sun, his energy reserves were depleted." *depletion (n.)* *deplere* to empty out: *de-* (expressing reversal) + *plere* to fill
expletive	**n.** an exclamation, oath, or swear word "Expletives are typically bleeped out on daytime television shows." *expletivus* serving to fill out or take up space: *ex-* out + *plere* to fill
implement	**v.** to put into effect **n.** a tool, utensil, or other piece of equipment "The legislature proposes laws, while the executive implements them." *implementation (n.)* *implere* to fill up; to satisfy (a task) < *im-* in + *plere* to fill
replete	**adj.** plentiful, abundant "The gangster's speech was replete with expletives." *replere* to fill again, to complete: *re-* back, again + *plere* to fill
incendiary	**adj.** causing or capable of causing fire; causing anger or outrage "The Molotov cocktail is an incendiary device consisting of gasoline in a wicked bottle." *incendiarism (n.)* *incendere* to set fire to; to provoke or excite
incense	**v.** to make very angry, to infuriate **n.** a gum, spice, or other substance that is burned for the sweet smell it produces "Sheila was incensed to learn of her husband's affair with the babysitter." *incendere* to set fire to; to provoke or excite
irascible	**adj.** easily made angry; hot-tempered; highly irritable "He frequently yelled at the nurses, because he was made irascible by constant pain."

	irascibility (n.) *irascibilis* < *ira* anger, resentment
irate	**adj.** extremely angry "The irate customer dashed off a furious letter to the company that wronged her." *ira* anger, resentment
circuit	**n.** a circular line, route, or movement "A circuit rider was a judge or minister who made the rounds of multiple towns." *circuitus* going around, encircled (past participle of the verb *circuire*, to go around: *circum-* around + *ire* to go)
circuitous	**adj.** longer than the most direct way "Instead of going by the most direct route, he followed a scenic and circuitous road." *circuitus* going around, encircled (past participle of the verb *circuire*, to go around: *circum-* around + *ire* to go)
itinerant	**adj.** traveling from place to place **n.** an itinerant person "Johnny Appleseed was an itinerant who planted trees up and down the Ohio Valley." *itinerari* to travel < *iter, itiner* journey, road
itinerary	**n.** a planned route of travel or journey "My travel itinerary includes Paris, Geneva, and Barcelona." *iter, itiner* journey, road
transit	**n.** the carrying of people or things from one place to another; an act of passing through or across a place "Forms of mass transit include trains, buses, and subways." *transire* to go across: *trans-* across + *itum* gone, moved (past participle of the verb *ire*)
transition	**n.** the process or period of changing from one condition to another "The Civil War marked the transition from a primarily agricultural economy to a more industrial one." *transire* to go across: *trans-* across + *itum* gone, moved (past participle of the verb *ire*)
transitory	**adj.** not permanent; short-lived "His headache proved transitory; the pain was gone in minutes." *transire* to go across: *trans-* across + *itum* gone, moved (past participle of the verb *ire*)

Exercise A

Fill in the blanks in the sentences below with the correct form of a word in the scroll above.

1. To finish the race, the cars had to complete 400 laps of the one-mile _____.

2. Sand that is wet has more _____ than dry sand and therefore is better for building sandcastles.

3. The family's travel _____ includes Cleveland, Chicago, and Michigan.

4. When the weekend carpenter hit his thumb with the hammer, he yelled an _____ that shocked his son.

5. On Halloween, the _____ old man was a favorite target for pranksters, who hid in the nearby woods to watch his furious reaction.

6. Her _____ kindness and generosity helped her make new friends with ease.

7. This glue provides strong _____ for woodworking joints.

8. The wise men gave frankincense and myrrh to the infant Jesus, which is why _____ is still used in formal church services.

9. It took many years of overfishing in Georges Bank area to _____ the fish stocks there.

10. His students made the _____ from high school to college easily, because he prepared them so well.

11. Before you apply paint, it is imperative to prepare the surface so that the new paint will _____ properly.

12. During World War II, when most professional athletes enlisted, _____ women's baseball teams toured the country.

13. The rock climber was hit in the head by falling debris, but he remained conscious and _____, and he was released from the hospital quickly.

14. The lawn mower replaced the sickle, an outdated farm _____.

15. Their _____ argument about the minimal impact of groundwater withdrawals was convincing to local officials.

16. The motorcycle rally used a _____ route through the countryside.

17. Anywhere there are _____ devices such as fireworks, it is wise to have a firetruck and an ambulance standing by.

18. The prisoner became _____ when the one of the guards accused him of going to the infirmary under false pretenses

19. He was once _____ with enthusiasm for his job as a lawyer for Child Protective Services, but he quit because he found it too emotionally draining.

20. Superglue is so _____ that you have to be careful not to get it between two fingers.

21. Although his time on earth was _____, he brought joy to his family, friends, and even the nurses who cared for him on the cancer ward.

22. The "T" subway in Boston is a popular form of mass _____.

Exercise B

Match the word with the letter of its definition.

1. ___ adhere
2. ___ adhesion
3. ___ circuit
4. ___ circuitous
5. ___ coherent
6. ___ cohesion
7. ___ deplete
8. ___ expletive
9. ___ implement
10. ___ incendiary
11. ___ incoherent
12. ___ inherent
13. ___ incense
14. ___ irascible
15. ___ itinerant
16. ___ itinerary
17. ___ irate
18. ___ replete
19. ___ transit
20. ___ transition
21. ___ transitory
22. ___ adhesive

a) an exclamation, oath, or swear word
b) permanent or essential to
c) a tool, utensil, or other piece of equipment
d) incomprehensible or confused
e) easily made angry; hot-tempered
f) the formation of a united whole
g) plentiful, abundant; filled with
h) a planned route of travel or a journey
i) extremely angry
j) to stick fast to
k) logical and consistent; understandable
l) roundabout, meandering
m) the process or period of changing from one condition or place to another
n) traveling from place to place
o) to reduce the number or quantity of; to drain
p) a circular line, route, or movement
q) to infuriate
r) the action or process of adhering
s) causing or capable of causing fire
t) the carrying of people or things from one place to another
u) impermanent; fleeting
v) sticky

Exercise C

Solve the crossword puzzle:

Across
4. a tool, utensil, or other piece of equipment
8. causing or capable of causing fire
15. to reduce the umber or quantity of; to drain
16. a planned route of travel or a journey
17. roundabout, meandering
20. impermanent; fleeting
21. easily made angry; hot tempered

Down
1. to infuriate
2. the carrying of people or things from one place to another
3. to stick fast to
5. the process or period of changing from on condition or place to another
6. incomprehensible or confused
7. logical and consistent; understandable
8. travelling form place to place
9. a circular line, route, or movement
10. extremely angry
11. plentiful, abundant; filled with
12. an exclamation, oath or swear word
13. the action or process of adhering
14. sticky
18. permanent or essential to
19. the formation of a united whole

Test 3

Choose the correct meaning for the underlined vocabulary word in each sentence.

1. "The good, by <u>affinity</u>, seek the good; the vile, by <u>affinity</u>, the vile. Thus of their own volition, souls proceed into heaven, into hell."

   The Divinity School Address by Ralph Waldo Emerson

   (a) unnatural attraction   (b) natural sympathy   (c) happenstance
   (d) complementarity   (e) magnetic attraction

2. "I will <u>confer</u> upon you the head of a fox, so that you may hereafter look as bright as you really are."

   The Road to Oz by L. Frank Baum

   (a) bestow   (b) show   (c) press   (d) preclude   (e) force

3. "And I do believe that you are not convinced – this I <u>infer</u> from your general character, for had I judged only from your speeches, I should have mistrusted you."

   The Republic by Plato

   (a) deduce   (b) wonder   (c) imply   (d) allude   (e) assume

4. "In order to obtain invariable physical laws, we have to proceed to differential equations, showing the direction of change at each moment, not the integral change after a <u>finite</u> interval, however short."

   The Analysis of Mind by Bertrand Russell

   (a) secret   (b) unknown   (c) limited   (d) wasted   (e) endless

5. "I will venture to <u>affirm</u>, that the three seasons wherein our corn has miscarried did no more contribute to our present misery, than one spoonful of water thrown upon a rat already drowned would contribute to his death...."

   The Prose Works of Jonathan Swift by Jonathan Swift

   (a) disagree   (b) declare to be true   (c) sympathize   (d) hope   (e) deny

6. "Also, Theodora tells me that your circumstances used to be much more affluent than they are at present."

   Poor Folk by Feodor Dostoyevsky

   (a) beneficial (b) forgiving (c) irregular (d) wealthy (e) simple

7. "… from the somewhat northern character of the flora in comparison with the latitude, I suspected that these islands had been partly stocked by ice-borne seeds, during the Glacial epoch."

   The Origin of Species by Charles Darwin

   (a) human population (b) wildlife (c) plants (d) perennials (e) location

8. "The bold attempt had miscarried by a fortuitous circumstance; and unless by some exceptional event, they could now never reach the moon's disc."

   Round The Moon by Jules Verne

   (a) planned (b) anticipated (c) unknown (d) accidental (e) courageous

9. "On the last occasion he had escaped by a forensic quibble and not, as usual, by a private escapade; and it was a question whether at the moment he was amenable to the law or not."

   The Man Who Knew Too Much by Gilbert K. Chesterton

   (a) fleeting and innocuous   (b) relating to evidence   (c) highly theoretical
   (d) quasi-scientific   (e) physically delicate

10. "If ever the fusion of two human beings into one has been accomplished on this sphere it was surely in their union."

    "The Awakening" and Selected Short Stories by Kate Chopin

    (a) spreading (b) merging (c) duplication (d) repeating (e) transferring

11. "Prose is a tardy genre, offspring of thought's distrust of the natural tendencies of language. Poetry belongs to all epochs; it is man's natural form of expression."

    The Bow and the Lyre by Octavio Paz

    (a) category (b) production (c) conglomeration (d) development
    (e) thought process

12. "The parsonage here's a tumble-down place, sir, not fit for gentry to live in."

    Adam Bede by George Eliot

(a) non-Jews (b) soldiers (c) upper class d. royalty (e) criminals

13. "Heidelberg lies at the mouth of a narrow gorge – a gorge the shape of a shepherd's crook; if one looks up it he perceives that it is about straight, for a mile and a half, then makes a sharp curve to the right and disappears."

A Tramp Abroad by Mark Twain

(a) hill (b) gully (c) field (d) ravine (e) slope

14. "But Nalasu had been famous as a great fighter, as well as having been the progenitor of three such warlike sons."

Jerry of the Islands by Jack London

(a) teacher (b) offspring (c) infant (d) enemy (e) father

15. "He remarks that, while the individual man is an insoluble puzzle, in the aggregate he becomes a mathematical certainty."

Sign of the Four by Sir Arthur Conan Doyle

(a) collective whole (b) official gathering (c) extraordinary circumstances
(d) extended family (e) company with subsidiaries

16. "He chatted for a moment with the officer, and then, bidding him good-night, walked on to his home, his mind in a whirl with conglomerate visions of buried cities, great grinning idols of gold, and rival professors seeking to be first at the goal."

Tom Swift In The Land Of Wonders by Victor Appleton

(a) temporary (b) separate (c) clustered (d) speedy (e) frightening

17. "He had made an egregious ass of himself before the whole ship."

The Innocents Abroad by Mark Twain

(a) well-known (b) outstandingly awful (c) dissolute (d) sociable
(e) likable

18. "The air grew cooler; they had surmounted the last gradient, and Oniton lay below them with its church, its radiating houses, its castle, its river-girt peninsula."

Howards End by E. M. Forster

(a) rooftop (b) slope (c) decline (d) extended (e) far-reaching

19. "Anyone could pick him at once as gregarious in his habits and communicative in his nature, with a quick wit and a ready smile."

The Valley of Fear by Sir Arthur Conan Doyle

(a) stubborn   (b) skilled   (c) confident   (d) sociable   (e) humorous

20. "As to the present situation of her mind, I shall <u>adhere</u> to a rule of Horace, by not attempting to describe it, from despair of success."

The History of Tom Jones, a Foundling by Henry Fielding

(a) listen   (b) admit   (c) stick fast   (d) submit   (e) disregard

21. "He was detestably poor, and this was the reason, no doubt, that his <u>expletive</u> expressions about betting, seldom took a pecuniary turn."

Poems by Edgar Allan Poe

(a) gracious   (b) exclamatory   (c) effective   (d) numerous   (e) offensive

22. "So too the poet, in representing men who are <u>irascible</u> or indolent, or have other defects of character, should preserve the type and yet ennoble it."

The Poetics of Aristotle by Aristotle

(a) not direct   (b) hopelessly inept   (c) uninformed   (d) easily angered   (e) selfish

23. "The one called Lucas was a mild and meek-looking little gentleman of clerical aspect; he had been an <u>itinerant</u> evangelist, it transpired, and had seen the light and become a prophet of the new dispensation."

The Jungle by Upton Sinclair

(a) fascinating   (b) frustrated   (c) traveling   (d) encouraging   (e) young

24. "The officer sends for Auersperg; these gentlemen embrace the officers, crack jokes, sit on the cannon, and meanwhile a French battalion gets to the bridge unobserved, flings the bags of <u>incendiary</u> material into the water, and approaches the tete-de-pont."

War and Peace by Leo Tolstoy

(a) flammable   (b) dirty   (c) aggravating   (d) dehydrated   (e) solid

25. "How grievous then was the thought that, of a situation so desirable in every respect, so <u>replete</u> with advantage, so promising for happiness, Jane had been deprived, by the folly and indecorum of her own family!"

Pride and Prejudice by Jane Austen

(a) oblivious   (b) obviously   (c) desperate   (d) abundant   (e) lacking

Lesson XXI

jac/jec, jocus, judico, junct/jug, jut/jurat

JAC, JEC
to throw

JOCUS
joke

JUDICO
to judge

JUNCT, JUG
to join

JUT, JURAT
to swear

abject, conjecture, ejaculatory, inject, interjection, projectile, trajectory, jocular, adjudicate, judicious, prejudice, adjunct, conjugal, conjunction, junction, juncture, subjunctive, abjure, conjure, jury, perjure

Word Definitions

abject	**adj.** hopeless; wretched; depressed as though cast away "The slums, filth, and cardboard shacks of Rio made for abject surroundings." *abicere* to reject: *ab-* away + *iacere/jacere* to throw
conjecture	**n.** an opinion or conclusion based on incomplete information; a guess "I was wrong in my conjecture that he was late because of a flat tire." *conicere* to put together (in thought): *con-* together + *iacere/jacere* to throw
ejaculatory	**adj.** said quickly and suddenly "The crowd at the bullfight let out ejaculatory gasps and 'Olés!' during the toreador's heart-stopping performance." *ejaculation (n.), ejaculate (v.)* *ejaculari* to dart out; to discharge: *ex-* out + *iacere/jacere* to throw
inject	**v.** to force liquid into a cavity; to throw into the midst of something "The porter in 'Macbeth' injects a note of humor into an otherwise gloomy drama." *injection (n.)* *inicere* to throw in: *in-* into + *iacere/jacere* to throw

LESSON XXI JAC/JEC, JOCUS, JUDICO, JUNCT/JUG, JUT/JURAT

interjection n. an exclamation; a remark interposed in a conversation
"Gene's interjection, 'Yikes!' echoed through the gallery."
interject (v.)
interiacere to interpose: *inter-* between + *iacere/jacere* to throw

projectile n. an object that can be thrown; a missile
"David's stone projectile struck Goliath in the temple and slew him."
proicere to throw forth: *pro-* forth + *iacere/jacere* to throw

trajectory n. the path described by a flying projectile; the course (something) traveled
"The bullet's trajectory showed he could not have killed himself."
traicere to throw across, to transfer: *trans-* across + *iacere/jacere* to throw

jocular adj. characterized by joking or wit
"Falstaff is Shakespeare's most famous jocular character."
iocus/jocus joke, game, sport

adjudicate v. to hear and settle by judicial procedure; to judge
"The Nuremberg judges adjudicated a dozen Nazis guilty of war crimes."
adjudicare to decree; to award or assign (judicially): *ad-* to, toward + *judicare* to judge

judicious adj. having or exhibiting sound judgment; prudent
"By judicious investments, even a person of moderate means can attain wealth."
judicare to judge

prejudice n. a preconceived preference or idea formed without reason or experience; a biased opinion
"He bought only French wines, showing a snobbish prejudice against California wines of equal quality."
praejudicium precedent, prejudgment: *prae-* in advance + *judicum* judgment

adjunct n. an additional and supplementary part; an assistant
"An adjunct professor teaches part-time and is not a full faculty member."
adjungere to attach, to join to: *ad-* toward + *jungere* to join

conjugal adj. relating to marriage or the relationship of spouses
"The new bride and groom spent the night in their conjugal bed."
conjungere to connect; to marry: *con-* together + *jungere* to join

conjunction n. two or more events occurring at the same time; a word used to connect clauses or sentences
"The employee's promotion came in conjunction with a salary increase."
coniungere to connect; to marry: *con-* together + *jungere* to join

junction n. the act or process of joining; a place where two roads, railroad lines, or other things join
"Meet me at the junction of 7th Avenue and 107th Street."
jungere to join

juncture	**n.** a point in time; a turning point or crisis; a joint or junction "It's now five o'clock. At this juncture, we will recess until nine tomorrow morning." *jungere* to join
subjunctive	**adj.** a verb tense expressing what is imagined, wished, or hoped for "Contrary-to-fact conditions require a grammatically subjunctive mood." *subjungere* to subjoin: *sub-* under, up to + *jungere* to join
abjure	**v.** to renounce under oath "Galileo abjured his heresy and denied his prior claim of a heliocentric universe." *abjurare* to repudiate; to deny under oath: *ab-* away + *iurare/jurare* to swear, to call to witness, to take an oath
conjure	**v.** to call to mind; to affect or produce as if through an incantation or spell; to practice magic "To be successful, a politician must be able to instantly conjure a plausible explanation for any dubious past votes." *conjurare* to swear or act together, to plot: *con-* together + *iurare/jurare* to swear
jury	**n.** a group of citizens sworn to judge a court case "The jury deliberated for four days before pronouncing him 'guilty.'" *iurare/jurare* to swear, to take an oath
perjure	**v.** to falsely swear; to lie under oath in court or another judicial forum "President Clinton was impeached on a perjury charge for lying about his sexual encounters with a White House intern." *perjury (n.)* *perjurare* to swear falsely: *per-* through + *iurare/jurare* to swear, to take an oath

Exercise A

Fill in the blanks in the sentences below with the correct form of a word in the scroll above.

1. Jesters were known as _____ entertainers who performed tricks for – and even poked fun at – kings and their courtiers.

2. The _____ of the skeet was so perfect that all the skeet shooters hit the flying target effortlessly.

3. _____ by white Americans toward racial and ethnic minorities has decreased significantly since the early 20th century.

LESSON XXI JAC/JEC, JOCUS, JUDICO, JUNCT/JUG, JUT/JURAT

4. The term "_____ poverty" refers to the state of impoverished communities where there's no hope of a better life.

5. Universities employ _____ faculty to supplement their tenure-track professors at lower cost.

6. When called to testify, the vagabond was afraid he would be forced to admit his own crimes, so he made up a story and _____ himself.

7. According to the Concise Oxford English Dictionary, the _____ is typically used in expressions such as, "Be that as it may be" or "Come what may."

8. The doctor may _____ you with a contrast dye before your CT scan, because the resulting images are much clearer and easier to read.

9. The word "and" serves as a _____ between two complete thoughts.

10. The scientist made a _____ about the way in which humans might be cloned by studying cloned goat embryos.

11. The school did not allow _____ in the classroom. However, it did sponsor a paper airplane contest outside on the playground.

12. Houdini used legerdemain to _____ objects, then make them disappear.

13. A twelve member _____ was sworn in before the trial began.

14. Alexander the Great had a _____ mind that enabled him to rule his vast kingdom intelligently and fairly.

15. The map indicates the exit at the _____ of Route 1 and Interstate 95.

16. Whenever they tried to have a serious conversation, their irrepressible son interrupted with one _____ after another.

17. In the "Newlyweds" TV show, Nick and Jessica are in a _____ relationship.

18. Oedipus attempted to _____ the argument between his wife and son.

19. Patients suffering from Tourette's Syndrome make _____ remarks, which may be disturbing or startling to those around them.

20. At the time of his resignation, Nixon was required to _____ all executive authority in the government of the United States.

21. At that _____, he saw no point in further argument and turned away.

143

Exercise B

Match the word with the letter of its definition.

1. ___ abject
2. ___ abjure
3. ___ adjudicate
4. ___ adjunct
5. ___ conjecture
6. ___ conjugal
7. ___ conjunction
8. ___ conjure
9. ___ ejaculatory
10. ___ inject
11. ___ interjection
12. ___ jocular
13. ___ judicious
14. ___ juncture
15. ___ junction
16. ___ jury
17. ___ prejudice
18. ___ perjure
19. ___ projectile
20. ___ subjunctive
21. ___ trajectory

a) an exclamation
b) to hear and settle by judicial procedure
c) said quickly and suddenly
d) a conclusion based on incomplete information
e) to deliberately lie under oath
f) a place where two railroad lines join
g) the path described by a flying projectile
h) an additional and supplementary part
i) an object that can be thrown or shot
j) two or more events occurring simultaneously
k) a preconceived preference or idea; a bias
l) wretched; hopeless
m) denoting a mood of verbs
n) to call to mind
o) characterized by joking
p) having or exhibiting sound judgment
q) to renounce under oath
r) relating to marriage
s) to force liquid into
t) a body of people sworn to give a verdict or judge a competition
u) a point in time; a crisis

Exercise C

Solve the crossword puzzle:

Across
5. a conclusion based on incomplete information
6. denoting a mood verbs
7. an additional and supplementary part
11. having or exhibiting sound judgement
13. said quickly and suddenly
14. wretched; hopeless
15. to deliberately lie under oath
16. to renounce under oath
17. an object that can be thrown or shot
19. two or more events occurring simultaneously

Down
1. an exclamation
2. to call to mind
3. characterized by joking
4. a preconceived preference or idea; a bias
5. relating to marriage
8. a point in time; a crisis
9. to force liquid into
10. to hear and settle by judicial procedure
11. a body of people sworn to give a verdict or judge a competition
12. the path described by a flying projectile
18. a place where two railroad lines join

Lesson XXII
labor, lateral, lavo/luo, leg, lego, lev

LABOR to work	***LATERAL*** side	***LAVO, LUO*** to wash
LEG law	***LEGO*** to send	***LEV*** light, rise

collaborate, laborious, collateral, equilateral, ablution, deluge, legal, legislature, legitimate, litigate, allegation, allege, legacy, legate, relegate, alleviate, elevate, leverage, levitation, levity

Word Definitions

collaborate **v.** to work jointly on an activity or project
"Rogers and Hammerstein, a lyricist and composer, collaborated on many musicals."
collaboration (n.)
collaborare to work together: *con-* together + *laborare* to work

laborious **adj.** requiring considerable time and effort
"Digging the 100-foot ditch was laborious."
labor (n.)
laborare to labor, to work < *labor, laboris* labor

collateral **adj.** situated or running side by side; parallel
n. something pledged as security for repayment of a loan; additional but subordinate
"The bomb not only destroyed the military target, but caused several civilian deaths, which the Army euphemistically called 'collateral damage.'"
collateralis collateral: *con-* together + *latus, lateris* side

equilateral **adj.** having all sides equal
"Seen head-on, a Swiss chalet has an equilateral façade."
aequilaterus equal-sided: *aequi-* equal + *latus, lateris* side

ablution **n.** washing the body
"He performed his ablutions using a basin of cold water from the well."

LESSON XXII LABOR, LATERAL, LAVO/LUO, LEG, LEGO, LEV

                    ablutionary (adj.)
                    abluere to wash away: *ab-* away + *luere* to wash

deluge   **v.** to overrun with water; to inundate
                n. a flood
                "The president was deluged with angry e-mails after the preemptive attack."
                diluere to wash away: *de-* down, away from + *luere* to wash

legal   **adj.** relating to, based on, or required by the law
                "Stealing bases is legal under the official baseball rules."
                legality (n.)
                lex, legis law, bill

legislature   **n.** an officially elected body vested with the power to make laws
                "The House of Lords and the House of Commons comprise the British legislature."
                legislate (v.)
                lex, legis law, bill

legitimate   **adj.** conforming to the law or to the rules; defensible with logic or justification; (of a child) born to a married couple
                "The eldest son born to the king and queen is the legitimate heir to the throne."
                legitimare to make legal < *legalis* legal, of the law

litigate   **v.** to engage in legal proceedings
                "The homeowner decided to litigate after the home contractor failed to fulfill their contract."
                litigation (n.)
                litigare to go to court < *lis, litis* lawsuit

allegation   **n.** an unproved assertion (under the law); something affirmed
                "His allegation was that the policeman had struck him, but that was refuted by eyewitnesses."
                allegare to allege, to suborn: *ad-* to + *legare* to deputize; to take to the law < *lex, legis* law

allege   **v.** to affirm or to assert without or before proof
                "The attorney alleged but couldn't prove that the defendant was lying."
                allegare to allege, to suborn: *ad-* to + *legare* to deputize; to take to the law < *lex, legis* law

legacy   **n.** an amount of money or property left to someone in a will; something intangible that has been bequeathed or inherited
                "His father's reputation as a ne'er-do-well was an unwanted legacy that hindered his own efforts to get ahead."
                legare to bequeath (under the law) < *lex, legis* law

legate   **n.** an official representative; an ambassador or messenger
                "The papal legate conveyed the church's antipoverty message to the

	economic forum." *legatus* envoy, ambassador, deputy, commander < *lex, legis* law
relegate	**v.** to assign an inferior rank or position to; to give a task to (someone); to banish "The rubbish was <u>relegated</u> to the trash pile." *relegation (n.)* *relegare* to banish, to remove: *re-* back + *legare* to bequeath; to deputize
alleviate	**v.** to make less severe; to ease "Aspirin and other analgesic medicines <u>alleviate</u> suffering." *alleviation (n.)* *allevare* to raise, to alleviate: *ad-* to, toward + *levare* to lighten, to lessen
elevate	**v.** to lift to a higher position "Eisenhower was <u>elevated</u> to the new rank of five-star general." *elevation (n.)* *elevare* to lift up < *ex-* out + *levare* to lighten, to lessen < *levis* light (in weight)
leverage	**n.** the action of a lever; something that conveys an advantage **v.** to gain an advantage; to employ (something) as a lever "He used his insider knowledge as <u>leverage</u> to negotiate a better deal. *levare* to raise, to lighten < *levis* light (in weight)
levitation	**n.** an apparent defiance of gravity "A Hovercraft floating on an air cushion seems to perform an act of <u>levitation</u>." *levitate (v.)* *levis* light (in weight)
levity	**n.** the treatment of a serious matter with humor or lack of due respect "Making jokes at his friend's expense was unpardonable <u>levity</u>." *levis* light (in weight)

Exercise A

Fill in the blanks in the sentences below with the correct form of a word in the scroll above.

1. People sometimes use friendships as _____ to gain employment.

2. To _____ that the death was a homicide rather than a suicide was premature, and ultimately proved incorrect.

3. A triangle with all three sides of equal length is called _____ .

4. According to the law, the homeowner's property claim was _____ .

5. After a remarkable victory, the colonel was _____ to major general.

6. The _____ to the Pope visited Jerusalem to meet with Christians who were eager for suggestions to end the dispute.

7. The moderator used _____ to regain the audience's attention, but some thought his jokes in poor taste.

8. The two scientists agreed to _____ on their chemistry experiments, and as a result, they shared the Nobel Prize.

9. Restaurant work is so _____ that there is a high staff turnover rate.

10. The businessman's _____ fees were threatening to bankrupt him, so he began to reconsider persevering in his lawsuit.

11. The lawyer attempted to _____ the children's distress by suggesting that their divorcing parents meet with a mediator.

12. Daily _____ in the Ganges River are a holy ritual for many Indians.

13. The father's _____ to his children was his home and his investments.

14. His mother posted a $100,000 bond, using her house as _____, to get him out of jail while he awaited trial.

15. After the inventor gave a radio interview, the station received a _____ of calls from listeners eager to learn more about his project.

16. A good leader has the ability to _____ lesser tasks to subordinates.

17. The newscaster was quick to correct himself, saying the police version of the shooting was an as-yet-unproven _____.

18. When the _____ goes into session, the tax bill will be the first order of business.

19. After she failed to budge in mediation, he decided he had no choice but to _____.

20. Magicians perform acts of _____, to the amazement of their audiences.

Exercise B

Match the word with the letter of its definition.

1. ___ ablution
2. ___ allegation
3. ___ allege
4. ___ alleviate
5. ___ collaborate
6. ___ collateral
7. ___ deluge
8. ___ elevate
9. ___ equilateral
10. ___ laborious
11. ___ legacy
12. ___ legal
13. ___ legate
14. ___ legislature
15. ___ legitimate
16. ___ leverage
17. ___ levitation
18. ___ levity
19. ___ litigate
20. ___ relegate

a) an unproved assertion
b) to work jointly on an activity or project
c) relating to, based on, or required by the law
d) to assign to an inferior rank or position
e) to engage in legal proceedings
f) conforming to the law or to the rules; justifiable
g) lightness of manner or speech; humor
h) a positional advantage
i) to affirm or assert without or before proof
j) the act of washing the body
k) to lift to a higher position; to promote
l) something bequeathed to someone
m) to make less severe; to lessen or soothe
n) a great quantity arriving at the same time; a flood
o) having all sides equal
p) an official representative or ambassador
q) situated side by side; security for a loan
r) an apparent defiance of gravity
s) requiring considerable time and effort
t) an officially elected body vested with the responsibility and power to make laws

Exercise C

Solve the crossword puzzle.

Across:
1. Money or property left to someone in a will or handed down by a predecessor. 3. Conforming to the law or to the rules; able to be defended with logic or justification. 5. The action of a lever; a positional advantage. 8. The treatment of a serious matter with humor or lack of due respect. 9. An officially elected body with the responsibility and power to make laws. 10. An unproved assertion. 12. To make less severe. 15. An official representative; an ambassador or messenger. 16. Having all sides equal. 17. Situated or running side by side; parallel; security for a loan. 19. To lift to a higher position. 20. The act of washing the body.

Down:
2. To work jointly on an activity or project. 4. Requiring considerable time and effort. 6. To assign an inferior rank, position, or task to (someone). 7. To flood with water or to inundate. 11. An apparent defiance of gravity. 13. Relating to, based on, or required by the law. 14. To affirm or assert without or before proof. 18. To contest or engage in legal proceedings.

Lesson XXIII
liber/ libr, liber, licencia, ligo, lingua, literal, loc

LIBER, LIBR-	***LIBER***	***LICENCIA***	***LIGO***
book	free	freedom	to bind

LINGUA	***LITERAL***	***LOC***	
tongue, speech	letter	place	

> *libel, libretto, liberal, liberation, libertine, liberty, illicit, license, licentious, league, ligation, ligature, lingual, linguistic, alliteration, literal, obliterate, locality, locus*

Word Definitions

libel **n.** the publication of a false statement that damages a person's reputation
"The outrageous tales in her tell-all biography led the subject to file a libel lawsuit."
libellus, libelli small book, pamphlet; libelous publication <

libretto **n.** the text of a dramatic musical work
"An English translation of the Italian opera's libretto was projected above the stage."
liber, libri book

liberal **adj.** having or giving freely; respectful and accepting of behavior or opinions different from one's own; ample
"The homeowner spread liberal amounts of fertilizer to assure a thick lawn."
liber free

liberation **n.** the act or process of achieving equal rights and status; the achievement of freedom after bondage, slavery, or oppression

LESSON XXIII LIBER/ LIBR, LIBER, LICENCIA, LIGO, LINGUA, LITERAL, LOC

"The Allies achieved the liberation of Paris from Nazi rule in early 1945."
liber free

libertine
n. an immoral person; a person who is freely indulgent in sensual pleasures; a free thinker in matters of religion
adj. characterized by disregard for morality
"Casanova was renowned as a libertine who seduced scores of women."
libertinism (n.)
libertinus freedman < *liber* free

liberty
n. freedom; the state of being free from oppression or imprisonment; (pl.) overly free or unrestricted actions
"The father warned the young man not to take any liberties with his underage daughter."
libertas freedom, ex-slave, outspokenness < *liber* free

illicit
adj. forbidden by law, rules, or custom
"The Mafia engaged in illicit activities like protection and numbers rackets."
illicitus not permitted, unlawful: *il-* not + *licitus* permitted < *licencia* freedom

license
n. 1) a permit from an authority to own or use something, do a particular thing, or carry on a trade; formal or official permission
n. 2) deviation from normal rules
v. to issue a license; to give someone formal permission to do something
"A poet will often take license with standard English usage to better express himself."
licentia freedom

licentious
adj. promiscuous and unprincipled (in sexual matters)
"Hookers frequent the Bois de Boulogne to carry out their licentious activities."
licentia freedom

league
n. a union of persons with common aims; a collection of people, countries, or groups that combine for mutual protection or cooperation
"The buccaneers were in league with Andrew Jackson at the Battle of New Orleans."
ligare to bind or tie

ligation
n. the act of binding or the state of being bound; the surgical procedure of tying a ligature tightly around an artery or vein
"The woman underwent a tubal ligation to prevent further pregnancies."
ligare to bind or tie

ligature
n. anything used to bind or tie up
"Surgeons used to rely on catgut or silk ligatures to sew up wounds."
ligare to bind or tie

lingual	**adj.** relating to or near the tongue; relating to speech or language "He grew up in a multi-lingual household; his parents spoke Spanish, English, and Russian." *lingua* tongue, language, speech
linguistic	**adj.** pertaining to language "His linguistic studies covered the neurological and environmental origins of language development." *lingua* tongue, language, speech
alliteration	**n.** repetition of the same sound at the beginning of words "In the phrase 'big, blue balloon' the initial 'b's' exemplify alliteration." *alliterate (v.)* *ad-* (expressing addition) + *littera* letter, something written
literal	**adj.** straightforward, not figurative; taking words in their concrete or usual sense; representing the exact words of the original text "The literal meaning of 'star' is a heavenly body; the figurative refers to a famous person." *littera* letter, something written
obliterate	**v.** to destroy utterly, to wipe out, erase "After Akhenaton's death, the priests obliterated the heretic's name from all the temples." *obliteration (n.)* *obliterare* to strike out, erase: *ob-* against + *littera* letter, something written
locale	**n.** a place associated with particular events "Gettysburg was the sole Northern locale of Civil War battles." *locus* place
locality	**n.** a particular neighborhood, place, or district; a specific place "It was in this locality that the series of brutal muggings took place." *localis* local < *locus* place
locus	**n.** the center of activity "Boston was the locus of early rebellion against England." *locus* place

Exercise A

Fill in the blanks in the sentences below with the correct form of a word in the scroll above.

1. The Major _____ Baseball Association employs only the best players.

2. Lucretia earned a reputation for _____ behavior because she was unfaithful to her husband.

LESSON XXIII LIBER/ LIBR, LIBER, LICENCIA, LIGO, LINGUA, LITERAL, LOC

3. West Andover is a _____ within the Town of Andover, but is not a separate political entity.

4. He was known as a wastrel and a _____ because he gambled away his family fortune – but not before getting some of the maidservants pregnant.

5. "Give me _____ or give me death" is a famous quote attributed to Patrick Henry at the time of the Revolutionary War.

6. The _____ for the musical was rewritten many times before the composer was satisfied.

7. Multi-lingual people may have studied _____ in-depth.

8. The surgeon performed the _____ of the arteries with great skill.

9. Abraham Lincoln's "Emancipation Proclamation" announced the _____ of all slaves in the Confederate states, but the reality took longer to achieve.

10. On weekends, the teenager liked to engage in _____ drinking, smoking, and other activities prohibited by his parents and his football coach.

11. The _____ of the federal government is Washington, D.C.

12. The witness in the _____ lawsuit testified to the falsehood of several purported "facts" included in the sloppy reporter's newspaper article.

13. Leaving house doors unlocked may seem to thieves a "_____ to steal."

14. "Amy always ate apples" is an example of _____.

15. The paramedics rushed to create a makeshift _____ out of gauze for the stabbing victim, who was bleeding heavily from an artery in his arm.

16. The _____ nerve was damaged during a dentist's injection of novocaine, and that side of the patient's tongue remained numb for months.

17. We considered several _____ before deciding on a Cape Cod inn as the perfect place for our wedding.

18. Julia Child sauced the entrée with a _____ helping of wine.

19. Thank goodness, the tornado did not _____ the town center, instead carving a narrow path on the outskirts.

20. A metaphorical description is quite opposed to a _____ presentation.

155

Exercise B

Match the word with the letter of its definition.

1. ___ alliteration
2. ___ illicit
3. ___ league
4. ___ libel
5. ___ liberal
6. ___ liberation
7. ___ libertine
8. ___ liberty
9. ___ libretto
10. ___ license
11. ___ licentious
12. ___ ligation
13. ___ ligature
14. ___ lingual
15. ___ linguistic
16. ___ literal
17. ___ locale
18. ___ locality
19. ___ locus
20. ___ obliterate

a) to destroy utterly, to wipe out
b) the process of achieving equal rights
c) formal or official permission (to do something)
d) the action of binding or tying tightly
e) a union of persons with common aims
f) the text of a dramatic musical work
g) pertaining to the study of languages
h) forbidden by law or the rules
i) taking words in their usual or concrete sense
j) a false, published statement that damages a person's reputation
k) the setting for particular events
l) freedom
m) anything used to bind or tie up tightly
n) promiscuous and unprincipled (of behavior)
o) the center of activity
p) having or giving freely
q) relating to the tongue or language
r) an immoral person
s) a particular neighborhood, place, or district
t) repetition of the same letter or sound at the beginnings of words

Exercise C

Solve the crossword puzzle:

Across
2. the text of a dramatic musical work
3. the center of activity
5. promiscuous and unprincipled (of behavior)
7. taking words in their usual or concrete sense
8. an immoral person
10. having or giving freely
11. to utterly destroy to wipe out
12. pertaining to the study of languages
13. forbidden by law or the rules
14. a particular neighborhood, place, or district
15. repetition of the same letter or sound at the beginnings of words

Down
1. formal or official permission (to do something)
2. the action of binding or tying tightly
3. the setting for particular events
4. the process of achieving equal rights
5. a union of persons with common aims
6. a false, published statement that damages a person's reputation
7. freedom
9. related to the tongue or language
12. anything used to bind or tie up tightly

Lesson XXIV
loqu/locut, luc/lum, ludo

LOQU, LOCUT
to talk

LUC, LUM
light

LUDO
to play

*colloquial, elocution, eloquent, loquacious, obloquy, soliloquy
elucidate, illuminate, lucent, lucid, luminary, luminescence, luminous,
pellucid, allude, allusion, collusion, delusion, elude, elusive*

Word Definitions

colloquial
adj. conversational or informal speech or writing (not formal or literary)
"'Colloquial' describes everyday spoken English as opposed to formal written English."
colloquium conversation: *co-* together + *loqui* to speak

elocution
n. the practice of clear and expressive speech, especially distinct pronunciation and articulation
"Demosthenes practiced speaking with pebbles in his mouth to hone his elocution."
eloqui to speak out: *ex-* out + *loqui, locut-* to speak

eloquent
adj. forceful and expressive
"The rows of graves in Arlington are eloquent testimony to American war sacrifices."
eloquence (n.)
eloqui to speak out: *ex-* out + *loqui* to speak

loquacious
adj. talkative
"My loquacious aunt rarely lets her husband get a word in edgewise."
loqui to speak

LESSON XXIV LOQU/LOCUT, LUC/LUM, LUDO

obloquy   **n.** public condemnation; disparaging language
"Saddam Hussein was subjected to obloquy by the Western media."
obloqui to interpose remarks, to interrupt: *ob-* against + *loqui* to speak

soliloquy   **n.** the act of speaking one's thoughts aloud while or as if alone, especially by a character in a play
"The 'To be or not to be' soliloquy finds Hamlet musing alone in a castle room."
soli- alone + *loqui* to speak

elucidate   **v.** to make clear; to explain
"The scientist elucidated his experimental method so all could understand it."
elucidation (n.)
elucidare to enlighten < *ex-* out + *lucidus* bright, shining, clear

illuminate   **v.** to light up; to make bright
"Buddha achieved spiritual illumination through lengthy contemplation."
lumen, luminis light
illumination (n.)
illuminatus lit up: *in-, il-* (expressing intensification) + *luminatus* brightened (past participle of the verb *lumare*, to brighten < *lumen, luminis* light, lamp, daylight

lucent   **adj.** emitting light, luminous; translucent or clear
"Fireflies are lucent insects that emit a pattern of flashes to attract mates."
lucere to shine < *lux, lucis* light, day, life

lucid   **adj.** easy to follow; clear
"As the general anesthesia wears off, it may take a while for the patient to become lucid again."
lucere to shine < *lux, lucis* light, day, life

luminary   **n.** a person who has achieved eminence or inspires others; a heavenly body that gives off light
"Several senators, world leaders, and Hollywood luminaries attended the banquet."
lumen, luminis lamp, light, day

luminescence   **n.** the emission of light by a substance that has not been heated or occurring at low temperatures
"Many plankton display luminescence, lending a cool glow to the nighttime ocean."
luminescent (adj.)
lumen, luminis lamp, light, day

luminous   **adj.** full of light
"A halo is a luminous arc painted around the heads of saints, angels, and the Holy Family in religious art."
lumen, luminis lamp, light, day

pellucid	**adj.** translucent and clear; easy to understand "The audience easily grasped his <u>pellucid</u> explanation of a tricky theory." *perlucere* to shine through: *per-* through + *lucere* to shine
allude	**v.** to hint at; to refer to (something) casually or indirectly "Shakespeare <u>alludes</u> to a number of Greek gods in plays like 'Romeo and Juliet.'" *alludere* to play around with: *ad-* toward + *ludere* to play, to tease
allusion	**n.** an indirect, casual, or implicit reference "His <u>allusion</u> to the guillotine brought to mind the terror of the French Revolution." *alludere* to play around with: *ad-* toward + *ludere* to play, to tease
collusion	**n.** secret or illegal cooperation in order to cheat or deceive others "A teller in <u>collusion</u> with the bank robbers opened the safe." *colludere* to act in collusion with: *con-* together + *ludere* to play
delusion	**n.** an idiosyncratic belief or impression that is not in accordance with a generally accepted reality; an incorrect idea or belief "Hitler's belief that Germany could quickly conquer England proved to be a <u>delusion</u>." *delude (v.)* *deludere* to deceive, to play false: *de-* from + *ludere* to play
elude	**v.** to evade or to escape, typically in a cunning or skillful way; to escape someone's comprehension or grasp "The Scarlet Pimpernel repeatedly <u>eluded</u> capture by the French revolutionaries." *eludere* to elude: *ex-* out, away + *ludere* to play
elusive	**adj.** difficult to find, catch, or achieve "Despite his determination, straight A's proved an <u>elusive</u> goal." *eludere* to elude: *ex-* out, away + *ludere* to play

Exercise A

Fill in the blanks in the sentences below with the correct form of a word in the scroll above.

1. Even though they had no savings, the newlyweds shared a vision – that their relatives called a _____ -- of living in splendor after their honeymoon.

2. The jewel thieves were able to _____ the police for months, but eventually they were caught.

3. He made an _____ to my struggling business in his speech, bringing a blush to my cheeks that was one part anger, one part shame.

LESSON XXIV LOQU/LOCUT, LUC/LUM, LUDO

4. The _____ of certain poster paints shows up when they are viewed under ultraviolet light.

5. Jane Fonda was subjected to public _____ and derided as 'Hanoi Jane' after she visited North Vietnam.

6. A _____ way of saying "Please move faster" is "Get the lead out."

7. Strategically placed streetlights help to _____ the highway at night.

8. The instructor's _____ explanation helped him understand the advantages of hand tools in cabinet building.

9. _____ people tend to annoy others who are trying to work quietly.

10. The stars in the desert sky were so _____ that they lit up the entire landscape.

11. Some people believe that resources such as Cliffnotes.com and Sparknotes.com help to _____ the more complex classics, such as James Joyce's *Ulysses*.

12. The two girls were in _____ , agreeing to tell their parents that they were doing homework, when actually they were shopping at the mall.

13. The classical radio host's _____ contained a trace of a British accent.

14. Initially, the teenager only _____ to his difficulties with math, but ultimately he decided to tell his parents that he had failed a test.

15. Among the numerous lecturers at the conference, there was only one real _____ : the famous astronomer Stephen Hawking, who was the keynote speaker.

16. A _____ in a play usually reveals the speaker's thoughts or an inner conflict.

17. Each of the pearls was a softly shining, perfectly _____ orb.

18. The graduation speech was so _____ that the speaker received a five-minute standing ovation.

19. He loved to gaze into her _____ eyes, which appeared to be perfect windows into her thoughts and emotions.

20. The _____ howler monkeys could be heard a mile away, but visitors to the Guatemalan jungle rarely see them in the leafy canopy.

Exercise B

Match the word with the letter of its definition.

1. ___ allude
2. ___ allusion
3. ___ colloquial
4. ___ collusion
5. ___ delusion
6. ___ elocution
7. ___ eloquent
8. ___ elucidate
9. ___ elude
10. ___ elusive
11. ___ illuminate
12. ___ loquacious
13. ___ lucent
14. ___ lucid
15. ___ luminary
16. ___ luminescence
17. ___ luminous
18. ___ obloquy
19. ___ pellucid
20. ___ soliloquy

a) talkative
b) the act of speaking one's thoughts aloud as if alone
c) clearly expressive (of speech or writing)
d) clear, easy to understand
e) to light up, to make bright
f) translucently clear
g) difficult to find, catch, or achieve
h) to hint at
i) giving off light
j) to make clear, explain
k) a person who inspires others
l) strong public condemnation
m) an indirect or implicit reference
n) a false and illogical belief
o) clear and expressive speech; good diction
p) used in ordinary or familiar conversation
q) shining
r) to cleverly escape or evade
s) secret or illegal cooperation
t) the emission of light by a substance that has not been heated

Exercise C

Solve the crossword puzzle.

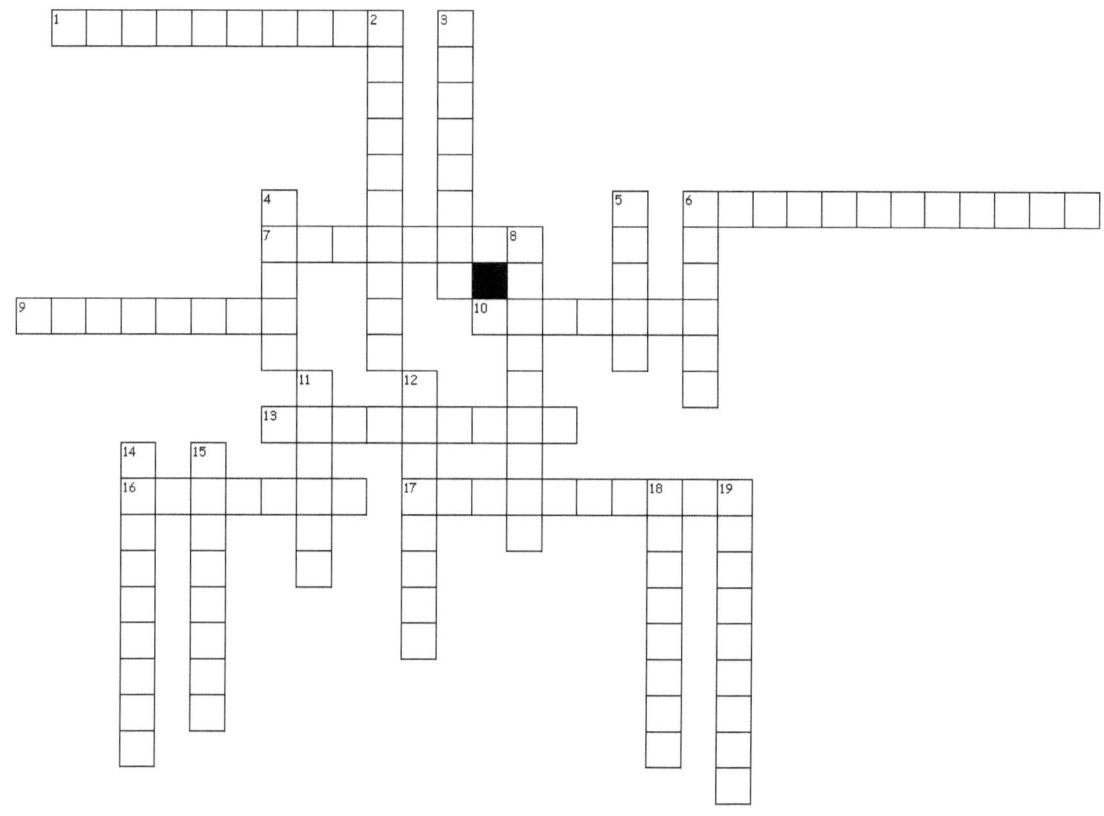

Across
1. used in ordinary or familiar conversation
6. the emission of light by a substance that has not been heated
7. giving off light
9. translucently clear
10. difficult to find, catch, or achieve
13. clear and expressive speech; good diction
16. strong public condemnation
17. to light up, to make bright

Down
2. talkative
3. a false and illogical belief
4. to cleverly escape or evade
5. clear, easy to understand
6. shining
8. the act of speaking one's thoughts aloud as if alone
11. to hint at
12. a person who inspires others
14. secret or illegal cooperation
15. clearly expressive(of speech or writing)
18. an indirect or implicit reference
19. to make clear; explain

Lesson XXV
man/manus, mar, mater/matr, medi

MAN, MANUS	*MAR*	*MATER, MATR*	*MEDI*
hand	sea	mother	middle

emancipate, mandate, mandatory, manifest, manipulate, manufacture, manuscript, cormorant, marinade, mariner, maritime, submarine, maternal, maternity, matriarch, matriculate, matrimony, matrix, mediate, medieval, mediocre

Word Definitions

emancipate　　**v.** to set free
"The animal rights activists <u>emancipated</u> the minks from the fur farm."
emancipare to emancipate: *ex-* out + *mancipare* to transfer property < *manus* hand + *capere* to take or seize

mandate　　**n.** an official order or command
"The Army <u>mandate</u> required all soldiers to shave their mustaches."
mandare to order; to entrust: *manus* hand + *dare* to give

mandatory　　**adj.** required by law, rule, or other obligation
"Military service was <u>mandatory</u> for all Spartan males from the age of 8 to 35."
mandare to order; to entrust: *manus* hand + *dare* to give

manifest　　**adj.** apparent to the eye or mind
v. to show (one's hand)
n. a document detailing a ship's contents, cargo, and passengers
"Heavy panting and a lagging gait made the marathon runner's fatigue <u>manifest</u>."
manifestus clear, blatant, obvious < *manus* hand

manipulate　　**v.** to handle or control with dexterity; to control or influence; to change to serve one's own ends

LESSON XXV MAN/MANUS, MAR, MATER/MATR, MEDI

"Dictators typically <u>manipulate</u> vote counting to guarantee their re-election."
maniple a handful; a company of soldiers: *manus* hand + (a word element of unknown origin)

manufacture   **v.** to make or process into a finished product; to fabricate
"The tardy student's excuse of a flat tire was <u>manufactured</u>."
manus hand + *facere* to make

manuscript   **n.** a handwritten or typed text; the unpublished version of a book or other written work
"Publishers turn authors' <u>manuscripts</u> into edited books."
manuscriptus handwritten: *manus* hand + *scriptus* written < *scribere* to write

cormorant   **n.** any of several diving marine birds
"A <u>cormorant</u> designates not only a diving water bird but also a greedy person."
corvus raven + *mar* sea

marinade   **n.** a liquid mixture with salt and other seasonings used to flavor or tenderize meat, fish, and other foods before cooking
"If you soak tough cuts of meat in an acidic <u>marinade</u> containing tomatoes or vinegar, it improves their taste and texture."
marinus of the sea < *mare, maris* sea

mariner   **n.** one who operates a ship; a sailor
"John Paul Jones was America's first commissioned <u>mariner</u> and naval officer."
marinus of the sea < *mare, maris* sea

maritime   **adj.** of, relating to, or along the sea
"The Canadian <u>Maritimes</u> is the name given to those provinces bordering the Atlantic Ocean."
maritimus of or near the sea; coastal

submarine   **n.** a vessel capable of operating submerged; something situated or living under the sea
"Torpedoes are missiles shot by <u>submarines</u> at underwater targets."
sub- under + *marinus* < *mare, maris* sea

maternal   **adj.** related through one's mother
"My mother's sisters and brothers are my <u>maternal</u> aunts and uncles."
mater mother

maternity   **n.** motherhood
adj. relating to pregnancy or motherhood
"Incubators for underweight newborns are found on the <u>maternity</u> ward."
maternus maternal < *mater* mother

matriarch	**n.** a woman who is head of the family; a woman who dominates a group "Queen Victoria was a long-reigning matriarch of 19th century Britain." *mater* mother
matriculate	**v.** to enroll as a student "Many graduating high school seniors matriculate three months later in college." *matriculare* enroll on a public register or list < *matrix* mother; list
matrimony	**n.** the rites of marriage; the state of being married "Holy matrimony is a sacred rite in the Roman Catholic Church." *matrimonius* matrimony, marriage < *mater* mother
matrix	**n.** an environment or material in which something develops; a grid or array that holds together smaller, disparate parts "A spider traps its prey in its web, which is a matrix of crisscrossing silk threads." *matrix, matricis* mother; female animal kept for breeding
mediate	**v.** to attempt or to bring about a compromise between conflicting sides "President Carter tried to mediate the conflict between Israel and the Palestinians." *medius* middle
medieval	**adj.** belonging to or having to do with the Middle Ages "Some Arab countries continue with medieval punishments, such as amputation of a hand for theft." *medius* middle
mediocre	**adj.** of average to inferior quality "The middle school students' mediocre performance on the standardized tests lowered the entire school district's state ranking." *mediocrity (n.)* *medius* middle

Exercise A

Fill in the blanks in the sentences below with the correct form of a word in the scroll above.

1. The high school senior hoped to _____ at an Ivy League school.

2. The publisher delivered the _____ to the printer on time to meet the publication deadline.

3. In comparison to Krispy Kreme doughnuts, Dunkin' Donuts treats are only _____.

LESSON XXV MAN/MANUS, MAR, MATER/MATR, MEDI

4. A _____ and several shipwrights were on board, the first to navigate, the latter to make any necessary repairs during the difficult voyage.

5. Once her baby was born, she could pack away her _____ clothes.

6. Most citizens in the north could more easily agree to _____ the slaves, since their economy was less dependent on large-scale farming.

7. Rose Kennedy was a "grande dame" and _____ of the Kennedy clan.

8. The business executives _____ the books to show greater sales revenues than they actually, artificially driving up the share price.

9. The divorcing couple asked their lawyers to help them _____ a settlement, so they wouldn't have a devastating court fight over child custody.

10. At most liberal arts colleges, writing classes are not optional, but _____.

11. The _____ for the fish was a mixture of fresh herbs, salt, white wine, and olive oil.

12. The toy company failed to _____ enough dolls to meet holiday demand.

13. It's fun to watch a _____ dive for fish, then sit on the rocks and spread its wings in the sun for warmth.

14. Many New England states sponsor a _____ academy to train those who wish to join the Coast Guard or make their living on the sea.

15. He did not obey his superior's _____ and was punished.

16. The little girl was devoted to her _____ grandmother, who often took care of her when her mother had to work late.

17. In _____ times, knights observed a strict code of chivalry toward their ladies.

18. The condemned man's courage was _____ in his refusal of a blindfold.

19. The biologist developed a _____ to grow artificial skin for burn patients from the victims' own cells.

20. _____ can be a big adjustment for older newlyweds who have been used to living on their own.

21. He took up scuba diving so he could study the development of _____ plants between the coral reefs and the shore.

Exercise B

Match the word with the letter of its definition.

1. ___ **cormorant**
2. ___ **emancipate**
3. ___ **mandate**
4. ___ **mandatory**
5. ___ **manifest**
6. ___ **manipulate**
7. ___ **manufacture**
8. ___ **manuscript**
9. ___ **marinade**
10. ___ **mariner**
11. ___ **maritime**
12. ___ **maternal**
13. ___ **maternity**
14. ___ **matriarch**
15. ___ **matriculate**
16. ___ **matrimony**
17. ___ **matrix**
18. ___ **mediate**
19. ___ **medieval**
20. ___ **mediocre**
21. ___ **submarine**

a) to enroll as a student
b) relating to the sea
c) any of several marine diving birds
d) motherhood
e) to control or influence cleverly
f) required by law or the rules
g) of average to inferior quality
h) one who operates a ship
i) to set free
j) an older woman who is the head of the family
k) apparent to the eye or mind; to show
l) to broker an agreement among conflicting parties
m) an official order or command
n) to fabricate
o) a liquid mixture used to flavor meat
p) belonging to the Middle Ages
q) related through one's mother
r) the rites of marriage
s) a handwritten or typed text
t) an environment or material in which something develops
u) living underwater; a vessel capable of submersion

Exercise C

Solve the crossword puzzle

Across

8. to enroll as a student
10. a handwritten or typed text
14. a liquid mixture used to flavor meat
15. related through one's mother
16. an environment or material in which something develops
19. to broker an agreement among conflicting parties

Down

1. to control or influence freely
2. apparent to the eye or mind; to show
3. one who operates a ship
4. living underwater; a vessel capable of submersion
5. rites of marriage
6. an official order or command
7. relating to the sea
8. motherhood
9. to set free
10. to fabricate
11. any of several marine diving birds
12. required by law or the rules
13. of average to inferior quality
17. an older woman who is the head of the family
18. belonging to the Middle Ages

Lesson XXVI

mel, mem/min, mendum, mereo, merg/mers, min

MEL
honey

MEM, MIN
to remember

MENDUM
defect

MEREO
to earn

MERG, MERS
dip, plunge

MIN
less

mellifluous, immemorial, memoir, memorabilia, memorandum, memory, reminiscent, emendation, mend, mendacious, mendicant, meretricious, meritorious, emerge, immersion, merge, submerge, minimal, minimize, minister, minute, minutia

Word Definitions

mellifluous adj. flowing like honey; smooth and sweet
"The lilting melody, delivered in her mellifluous voice, charmed the audience."
mellifer honey-producing: *mel, mell-* honey + *fluere* to flow

immemorial adj. timeless, extending beyond memory; a very old or long past
"'Since time immemorial' is used to describe a state of affairs that has existed longer than anyone can remember."
immemoris forgetful, lacking memory; heedless: *in-* not + *memor, memoris* mindful, remembering

memoir n. an autobiography; an account of an author's personal experiences
"Both Clintons have published best selling memoirs."
memoria memory, recollection, history < *memor, memoris* mindful, remembering

memorabilia n. objects kept or collected because of their associations with memorable people or events
"Souvenirs are often memorabilia of places we have visited."
memorabilis memorable

LESSON XXVI MEL, MEM/MIN, MENDUM, MEREO, MERG/MERS, MIN

memorandum   n. a written message in business or diplomacy; a brief note (**memo** is the more common, shortened form of the word)
"A memorandum of understanding is a brief note that, properly drafted, may serve as a contract."
memorandum memorandum < *memorare* to note; to remind or recount

memory   n. the mental faculty of retaining and recalling past experience
"'Memory' is the capacity of men or machines to embed and later retrieve information."
memorize (v.)
memor, memoris mindful, remembering

reminiscent   adj. recalling the past; tending to remind one of something
"Kennedy's 'New Frontier' speech was reminiscent of America's pioneering days."
reminisce (v.)
reminiscens call to mind: *re-* again + *memini* remember < *mens* mind

emendation   n. an alteration intended to improve
"Editors are expected to make emendations to manuscripts with faulty grammar or spelling."
emendare to correct or repair: *ex-* out of + *mendum, mendi* defect, fault

mend   v. to restore to a sound condition; to improve (shortening of amend)
"'Mending fences' means to make up for past disputes and become friendly again."
mendum, mendi defect, fault

mendacious   adj. not truthful, lying
"Mendacious medicine peddlers in the Old West misrepresented the healing powers of their wares."
mendacium lie, falsehood < *mendax, mendacis* lying, counterfeit

mendicant   n. a person who begs for a living; a beggar
"St. Francis' vow of poverty led to a mendicant's life, in which he was dependent on others for food."
mendicare to beg < *mendicus* beggarly, pitiful < *mendum* (physical) defect, fault

meretricious   adj. attracting attention in a vulgar manner; insincere, or based on deception
"With garish make-up and micro-miniskirts, the prostitutes were a meretricious bunch."
meretrix, meretric prostitute, courtesan < *merere* to earn pay

meritorious   adj. deserving reward or praise; having merit
"The Medal of Freedom is awarded for meritorious service to the United States."
meritorius hired, earning money < *merere* to earn pay

emerge   v. to come forth out of (something)
"The lucky soldier emerged unscathed from the battle."

	emergence (n.) *emergere* to rise up out of the water: *e-* out, forth + *mergere* to plunge, to immerse
immersion	**n.** the act of covering completely in liquid; complete absorption in a situation or subject "The Army uses the immersion method to teach languages." *immergere* to dip into: *in-* into + *mergere* to plunge
merge	**v.** to combine or be combined into a single entity "An amphicar merges a boat and an automobile into a single vehicle." *mergere* to plunge, to immerse
submerge	**v.** to be or cause to be underwater "The battleship Indianapolis, sunk in World War II, remains submerged on the ocean floor." *submergere* to plunge under: *sub-* under + *mergere* to plunge
minimal	**adj.** the least amount; of the smallest amount, quantity, or degree "U.S. citizenship and 35 years of age are minimal requirements to run for the federal office." *minimus* small, little
minimize	**v.** to reduce to the least or smallest size "A flu shot should minimize your chances of coming down with the disease." *minimus* small, little
minister	**n.** a head of a government department; a member of the clergy **v.** to care for someone or serve their needs "Florence Nightingale ministered to wounded English soldiers in the Crimean War." *minister* servant, aide < *minus, minime* less, not so good
minute	**adj.** extremely small "Even a minute speck of dust is enough to corrupt a microchip during manufacture." *minutus* made small < *minuere* to lessen
minutia	**n.** a small or trivial detail; the small or precise details of something "The chief financial officer tends to the company's large-scale financial wellbeing; the certified public accountant handles the minutia." *minutia* smallness < *minutus* made small

Exercise A

Fill in the blanks in the sentences below with the correct form of a word in the scroll above.

1. The CEO sent out a _____ to review before the meeting.

LESSON XXVI MEL, MEM/MIN, MENDUM, MEREO, MERG/MERS, MIN

2. The baby chicks should _____ from their eggs in a few days.

3. The Dalai Lama, in his philosophical texts, says that we should not waste our time on the _____ in life, but work toward greater goals such as inner peace.

4. The _____ suspect gave an alibi that the police were later able to disprove.

5. The _____ was caught in a traffic jam and arrived late to the church.

6. The Hopi have performed ceremonies in these kivas from time _____.

7. Botox injections can _____ wrinkles by paralyzing the tiny muscles that cause them.

8. The doctor's award for _____ service was presented at the annual meeting.

9. Sports fanatics often collect _____ of their favorite teams.

10. After much deliberation, the two local banks decided to _____ so as to withstand competition from larger, regional banks.

11. The editor's _____ significantly improved the essay.

12. The Cyclone at Six Flags is _____ of the old wooden roller coaster at Coney Island.

13. The _____ quality of Sarah Brightman's soprano voice made her the ideal muse for Andrew Lloyd Webber.

14. When they grow older, movie stars often write _____ about their exciting careers, interspersed with details of their private lives and Hollywood gossip.

15. Jesus was baptized by _____ in the Jordan River.

16. In some impoverished countries, some people deliberately cripple themselves so as to earn their living as _____.

17. The woman quickly decided the _____ fashions in Frederick's of Hollywood were really not to her taste; even Victoria's Secret made her blush.

18. "To take a trip down _____ lane" is to indulge in pleasant or sentimental memories.

19. A person used to public speaking can prepare a speech with _____ practice time, but I need at least a week.

20. There were _____ hairs allover his clothing from sitting on the cat's favorite chair.

21. After skiing, he _____ everything but his head in the hot tub, hoping to ward off stiff muscles the next day.

22. I told him to _____ his ways, or I would fire him.

Exercise B

Match the word with the letter of its definition.

1. ___ emendation
2. ___ emerge
3. ___ immemorial
4. ___ immersion
5. ___ mellifluous
6. ___ memoir
7. ___ memorabilia
8. ___ memorandum
9. ___ memory
10. ___ mend
11. ___ mendacious
12. ___ mendicant
13. ___ meretricious
14. ___ merge
15. ___ meritorious
16. ___ minimal
17. ___ minimize
18. ___ minister
19. ___ minute
20. ___ minutia
21. ___ reminiscent
22. ___ submerge

a) something remembered
b) attracting attention in a vulgar manner
c) small or trivial details
d) to reduce to the least or smallest possible
e) timeless, extending beyond memory
f) deserving reward or praise
g) tending to remind (someone of something)
h) to combine to form a single entity
i) an alteration intended to improve; a correction
j) extremely small
k) a brief, written message in business or diplomacy
l) a person who begs for a living
m) to come into existence or prominence
n) to cover completely with liquid
o) a member of the clergy
p) untruthful
q) pleasantly smooth and musical
r) the least possible
s) an autobiographical account
t) objects kept due to their associations with memorable people or events
u) to fix something broken
v) to go or cause to be placed under water

Exercise C

Solve the crossword puzzle

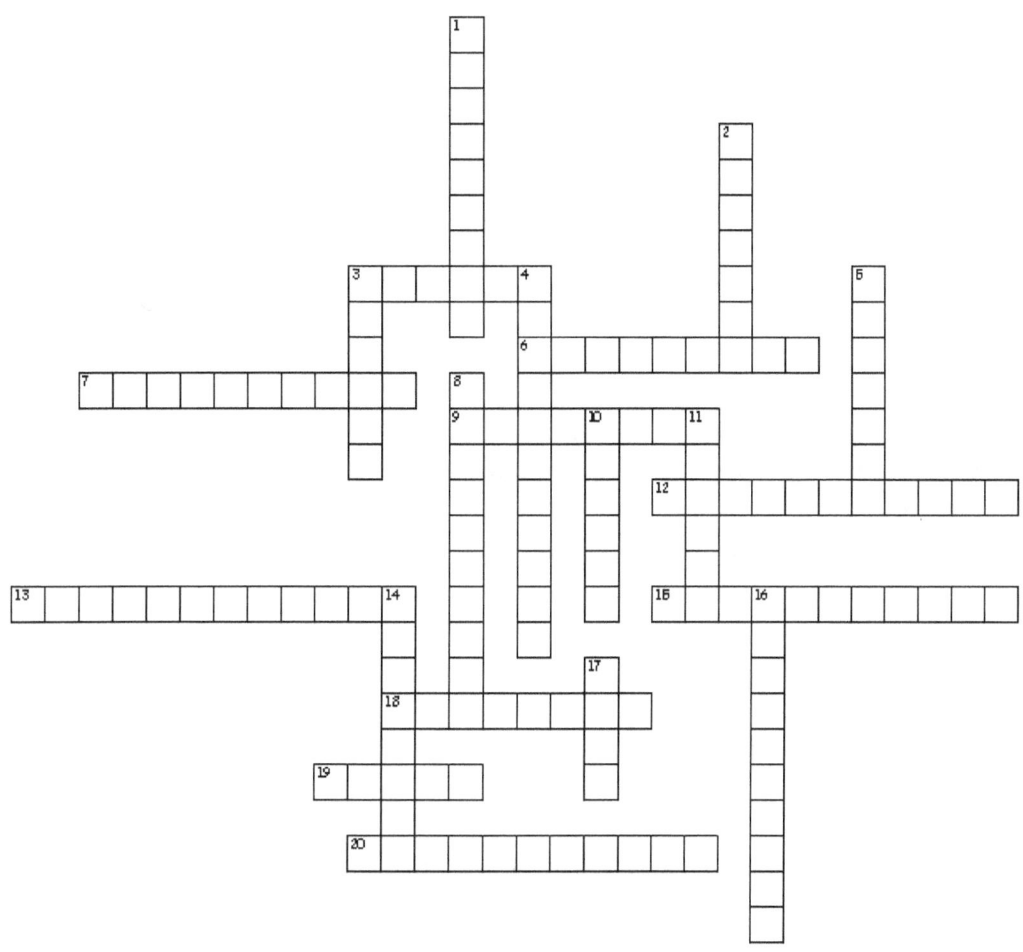

Across
3. An autobiography; an account of someone's personal experiences. 6. A person who seeks alms (often religious); a beggar. 7. Not truthful, lying. 9. To reduce to the least or smallest possible. 12. Flowing like honey; smooth and sweet. 13. Attracting attention in a vulgar manner. 15. Deserving reward or praise; having merit. 18. A head of a government department; a member of the clergy. 19. To combine or be combined to form a single entity. 20. Objects kept or collected because of their associations with memorable people or events.

Down
1. Complete absorption in a situation or subject; covered completely in liquid. 2. The small or precise details of something. 3. Extremely small. 4. Recalling the past; tending to remind (someone of something). 5. The least possible; of a minimum amount, quantity, or degree. 8. The act of correcting a defect or mistake; an alteration intended to improve. 10. The mental faculty of retaining and recalling past experience. 11. To come out of something into visibility or prominence. 14. To go or be put under water. 16. Timeless, extending beyond memory; very old or long past. 17. Abbreviation for a written message in business or diplomacy.

Lesson XXVII
mit/miss, mob/mot/mov

MIT, MISS
to send

MOB, MOT, MOV
to move

admit, admittance, commit, demise, emissary, emission, emit, missile, missive, permission, permissive, permit, premise, promise, remit, submit, transmit, immovable, mobilize, moment, momentum, motion, remote

Word Definitions

admit
v. to permit to enter; to accept; to confess
"Erica was admitted to a prestigious high school."
admittere to admit: *ad-* toward + *mittere* to send

admittance
n. permission or right to enter
"Her letter of admittance came three days before her birthday."
admittere to admit: *ad-* toward + *mittere* to send

commit
v. to give something for safe keeping; to agree to do something
"I would love to go with you on Sunday, but I have already committed to attend my brother's soccer game."
committere to join, entrust: *con-* with + *mittere* to send

demise
n. a death which causes the transfer of an estate; the end or failure of something
"The invention of the CD player led to the demise of cassette tapes."
dimittere: dis- away + *mittere* to send

emissary
n. a person sent as a messenger to represent or advance the interests of others
"The United States sent emissaries to the Middle East to persuade both

LESSON XXVII MIT/MISS, MOB/MOT/MOV

Israeli and Arab leaders of the benefits of negotiation."
emittere to send out: *ex-* out + *mittere* to send

emission   **n.** the act or instance of emitting; (pl.) air pollution
"Power plant <u>emissions</u> are being more strictly monitored because they contribute to global warming."
emittere to send out: *ex-* out + *mittere* to send, to throw

emit   **v.** to give off; to discharge; to send out
"As a meteor progresses through our atmosphere it burns up and <u>emits</u> light, creating the phenomenon known as a shooting star."
emittere to send out: *ex-* out + *mittere* to send, to throw

missile   **n.** an object that is fired, thrown, dropped, or otherwise projected at a target; a projectile
"There is an international ban on intercontinental ballistic <u>missiles</u>."
mittere to send, to throw

missive   **n.** a written message; a letter
"Please deliver this <u>missive</u> to my lovely wife in Geneva."
mittere to send

permission   **n.** consent, authorization
"The boy left home without <u>permission</u> from his mother, and now he must face the consequences."
permittere to permit: *per-* through + *mittere* to send

permissive   **adj.** granting or inclined to grant permission; tolerant, lenient
"My father is more <u>permissive</u> than my strict mother."
permittere to permit: *per-* through + *mittere* to send, to release

permit   **v.** to allow; to grant leave or consent
n. an official document allowing something
"You must get a building <u>permit</u> from the town before beginning construction."
permittere: *per-* through + *mittere* to send, to release

premise   **n.** a statement assumed to be true; an underlying assumption; a hypothesis; (plural) a piece of property owned by a person or business
"The <u>premise</u> of my movie is that humans are intrinsically devious."
praemittere to send ahead or forward: *prae-* before + *mittere* to send

promise   **n.** a written or spoken statement binding a person to an action
"I <u>promise</u> to tell the truth."
promittere to put forth, to promise: *pro-* before + *mittere* to send

remit   **v.** to refrain from exacting or inflicting (a tax, a punishment); to send (in payment) or send back; to restore to a previous position or state
"He promised to <u>remit</u> the money within two weeks."
remittere to send back, restore: *re-* back + *mittere* to send

submit	**v.** to yield control to someone or something "I submit myself to your authority; you have proved the worthier man." *submittere*: *sub-* under + *mittere* to send
transmit	**v.** to cause to pass from one place or person to another; to broadcast or send out "The radio station transmits its signal at 50,000 watts." *transmittere* to send or go across: *trans-* across + *mittere* to send
immovable	**adj.** not able to be relocated or changed "The base of the rock was so deeply buried it proved immovable." *in-* not + *movere* to move
mobilize	**v.** to prepare or organize for active service or for a particular task "In preparation for the impending attack, the troops mobilized." *mobile, mobilis* moveable
moment	**n.** a very brief period of time; importance or consequence; a particular time (in history) "For a moment, I thought the woman was my dead aunt, but I realized immediately that she couldn't be." *momentum* moment; movement
momentum	**n.** the impetus gained by a moving object "Trains build great momentum and cannot stop quickly" *momentum* moment; movement
motion	**n.** the action or process of moving or being moved "The motion of the boat caused me to become seasick." *motus* movement
remote	**adj.** far off; far away in space or time "The remote control for a television allows one to control the TV from afar." *removere* to move back, put away, withdraw: *re-* back + *movere* to move

Exercise A

Fill in the blanks in the sentences below with the correct form of a word in the scroll above.

1. The _____ of the roller-coaster left him nauseated and dizzy.

2. It was necessary to _____ him to a mental hospital because the doctors deemed him a danger to himself.

3. Based on the _____ that the applicant was intelligent and well-prepared, she was placed in an advanced course of study.

LESSON XXVII MIT/MISS, MOB/MOT/MOV

4. In a dictatorship, everyone must _____ to the rule of the leader.

5. After launch, the _____ is monitored by NASA with ground radar.

6. Following _____ of the Soviet Union, Russia stayed a world power.

7. The judge agreed to _____ her jail sentence if she performed 200 hours of community service.

8. Her parents are so _____ that they allow her to stay out as late as she wants, even on school nights.

9. He _____ to the crime in a telephone call that police were recording.

10. She proved _____ on the matter of salary, so he had to decide how badly he wanted the job.

11. The sled's _____ caused the child to crash into a fence.

12. The _____ came when he needed to act decisively or lose her.

13. The town would not _____ the protesters to assemble in the central square, but relegated them to a spot two blocks from the courthouse.

14. He sent a _____ to his fiancee, reassuring her of his love.

15. To halt industrial espionage, no _____ is granted the general public.

16. An American ex-president or respected politician can be an effective _____ , even if he or she has no official standing.

17. The ship's communications officer was scheduled to _____ an encoded message as soon as he made contact with the shore patrol.

18. The general decided to _____ his troops for a two-pronged assault.

19. The recluse now lives in a _____ cottage in rural Maine.

20. The light bulb might _____ a shower of sparks when it breaks.

21. He gave them _____ to use the theater when the play wasn't being rehearsed.

22. His blather was nothing more than the _____ of hot air.

23. He made a solemn _____ under oath to tell the whole truth.

Exercise B

Match the word with the letter of its definition.

1. ___ admit
2. ___ admittance
3. ___ commit
4. ___ demise
5. ___ emissary
6. ___ emission
7. ___ emit
8. ___ immovable
9. ___ missile
10. ___ missive
11. ___ mobilize
12. ___ moment
13. ___ momentum
14. ___ motion
15. ___ permission
16. ___ permissive
17. ___ permit
18. ___ premise
19. ___ promise
20. ___ remit
21. ___ remote
22. ___ submit
23. ___ transmit

a) a written message; a letter
b) to allow; to grant leave or consent
c) the process or right to enter
d) the process or result of emitting something
e) to assemble for active service
f) the impetus gained by a moving object
g) not able to be moved or changed
h) to give something (to someone) for safe keeping
i) a projectile
j) to refrain from exacting or inflicting
k) to permit to enter; to confess
l) a person sent as a messenger
m) the action or process of moving
n) the end or failure of something; death
o) consent; authorization
p) tending to permit
q) to give off; to discharge
r) a written or spoken statement binding someone to an action
s) a very brief period of time
t) a statement assumed to be true; a hypothesis
u) far away in space or time
v) to broadcast or send out
w) to yield control to someone or something

Exercise C

Solve the crossword puzzle

Across
4. the action or process of moving
5. to refrain from exacting or inflicting
9. the impetus gained by a moving object
11. not able to be moved or changed
13. to allow; to grant leave or consent
14. a written message; a letter
15. projectile
16. far away in space or time
17. a statement assumed to be true; a hypothesis
18. to give off; to discharge
19. to yield control to someone or something
20. to permit to enter; to confess

Down
1. the process or right to enter
2. to give something (to someone) for safe keeping
3. consent; authorization
6. to broadcast or sent out
7. to assemble for active service
8. the end or failure of something; death
10. a written or spoken statement binding someone to an action
12. a very brief period of time
18. a person sent as a messenger

Test 4

Choose the correct meaning for the underlined vocabulary word in each sentence.

1. "But the words were hardly uttered, before the smile was struck out of his face and succeeded by an expression of such <u>abject</u> terror and despair, as froze the very blood of the two gentlemen below."
   Dr. Jekyll and Mr. Hyde by Robert Louis Stevenson

   (a) pleasant   (b) hopeless   (c) forced   (d) incomplete   (e) sudden

2. "Once a man has lost his self-respect, and has decided to <u>abjure</u> his better qualities and human dignity, he falls headlong, and cannot choose but do so."
   Poor Folk by Fyodor Dostoyevsky

   (a) settle   (b) denote   (c) forswear   (d) judge   (e) call for

3. "My way led through Pleasant Meadow, an <u>adjunct</u> of the Baker Farm, that retreat of which a poet has since sung…"
   Walden & on the Duty of Civil Disobedience by Henry David Thoreau

   (a) joined but subordinate   (b) the main object   (c) outside one's experience
   (d) an interior exhibit   (e) next door to

4. "'The soldiers say it feels easier without boots,' said Captain Tushin, smiling shyly in his uncomfortable position, evidently wishing to adopt a <u>jocular</u> tone."
   War and Peace by Leo Tolstoy

   (a) forced   (b) quiet   (c) exclaiming   (d) prudent   (e) joking

5. "The millmen resolved to bestow public honors on Dominicus Pike, only hesitating whether to tar and feather him, ride him on a rail, or refresh him with an <u>ablution</u> at the town pump, on the top of which he had declared himself the bearer of the news."
   From Twice Told Tales by Nathaniel Hawthorne

   (a) measure   (b) drink   (c) pitcher   (d) washing   (e) ointment

6. "The Locrians were laid waste by a <u>legate</u> of Scipio, yet they were not avenged by him, nor was the insolence of the <u>legate</u> punished, owing entirely to his easy nature."

The Prince by Nicolo Machiavelli

(a) peasant (b) farmer (c) official emissary (d) personage
(e) nobleman

7. "'Why, <u>elevate</u> your own servants, for a specimen,' said Alfred, with a half-scornful smile."

Uncle Tom's Cabin by Harriet Beecher Stowe

(a) ease (b) promote (c) arrange (d) treat with respect
(e) give payment

8. "…and why should I not have some comrade with me to divide its dangers and <u>alleviate</u> its hardships?"

Typee by Herman Melville

(a) encourage (b) assist (c) raise (d) defy (e) ease

9. "Biographical historians and historians of separate nations understand this force as a power <u>inherent</u> in heroes and rulers."

War and Peace by Leo Tolstoy

(a) intrinsic (b) confusing (c) abundant (d) conferred (e) reduced

10. "I could see Macdona among the doctors – 'Hope in Harley Street' – Mac had always a weakness for <u>alliteration</u>."

The Poison Belt by Sir Arthur Conan Doyle

(a) straight forward (b) tied up (c) pertaining to foreign languages
(d) repetition of a sound at beginning of words (e) slurring speech

11. "'The extracts from my son's diary are a <u>libel</u> on his character,' she said."

Law and the Lady by Wilkie Collins

(a) creditable remark (b) overly free opinion (c) false disparagement
(d) flattering comment (e) violent assault

12. "In his youth he had been a dissolute <u>libertine</u>, but was converted by Mother Ann herself, and had partaken of the wild fanaticism of the early Shakers."

Twice Told Tales by Nathaniel Hawthorne

(a) philanderer (b) revolutionary (c) free person (d) alcoholic
(e) government official

13. "She makes no secret of them, and has, in fact, elaborated a complete system of <u>licentious</u> behaviour."

A Bundle of Letters by Henry James

(a) unlawful   (b) promiscuous   (c) forbidden   (d) binding   (e) sadistic

14. "It would almost seem as if Nature herself had tried to <u>obliterate</u> the evil signs of what had occurred."

The Lair of the White Worm by Bram Stoker

(a) retain   (b) display   (c) obscure   (d) support   (e) erase

15. "His rhetoric there, and in certain of his historical studies, had a sort of luminous richness, without losing its <u>colloquial</u> ease."

My Literary Passions by William Dean Howells

(a) expressive   (b) conversational   (c) talkative   (d) skillful   (e) lowbrow

16. "As he became aware that she was listening closely, he grew still more <u>eloquent</u> in his descriptions of various happenings in his career."

Maggie: A Girl of the Streets by Stephen Crane

(a) exacting   (b) exciting   (c) expressive   (d) flowery   (e) experimental

17. "I was willing to encounter some risks in order to accomplish my object, and counted much upon my ability to <u>elude</u> these prowling cannibals amongst the many coverts which the mountains afforded."

Typee by Herman Melville

(a) evade   (b) hint at   (c) fill with wonder   (d) maintain, keep constant   (e) satisfy

18. "So they <u>emancipate</u> themselves, break the yoke of the architect, and take themselves off, each one in its own direction."

Notre-Dame de Paris by Victor Hugo

(a) handle   (b) command   (c) liberate   (d) control   (e) process

19. "He thought he lived in a country where turkeys were the ruling class, and every year they held a feast to <u>manifest</u> their sense of Heaven's goodness in sparing their lives to kill them later."

Fantastic-Fables by Ambrose Bierce

(a) obligate   (b) officially order   (c) fabricate   (d) demonstrate   (e) handwrite

20. "Manson Mingott, the <u>Matriarch</u> of the line, would dare."

The Age of Innocence by Edith Wharton

(a) female head of family (b) commander-in-chief (c) self-sacrificing mother
(d) woman operating a ship (e) male progenitor

21. "He painted studies from nature under the guidance of an Italian professor of painting, and studied medieval Italian life."

Anna Karenina by Leo Tolstoy

(a) ancient and religious (b) exceptional (c) belonging to the Middle Ages
(d) everyday, average (e) modern and refined

22. "In the meantime they were advancing toward the square, and the moment the coadjutor and the curate put their feet on the first church step the mendicant arose and proffered his brush."

Twenty Years After by Alexandre Dumas

(a) nobleman (b) beggar (c) royalty (d) farmer (e) clergyman

23. "Such behaviour as this, so exactly the reverse of her own, appeared no more meritorious to Marianne, than her own had seemed faulty to her."

Sense and Sensibility by Jane Austen

(a) vulgar (b) covering completely (c) malicious and false
(d) praiseworthy (e) attracting attention

24. "At last I ran away myself, whenever I saw an emissary of the police approaching with some new intelligence; and lived a stealthy life until he was tried and ordered to be transported."

David Copperfield by Charles Dickens

(a) disguise (b) estate (c) discharge (d) service (e) agent

25. "I broke the seal with a great effort – so great a one that I was a long time coming to it; took the unopened missive at last up to my room and only attacked it just before going to bed.

Turn Of The Screw by Henry James

(a) permit (b) package (c) letter (d) prayer-book (e) meal

Appendix A
Quizzes

Quiz 1: Chapters 1-5

Agility, Alien, Aperture, Annuity, Artificial, Avuncular
Incantation, Recalcitrant, Carnivorous, Cerebral

1. "The same may be said of the other _____ lakes full of ships that go in and out upon this high road to all parts of the world." *The Mirror of the Sea* by Joseph Conrad

2. "I am not myself prepared to go farther than to say in general terms that we have almost certainly been in contact to-night with some form of _____ dinosaur." *The Lost World* by Sir Arthur Conan Doyle

3. "Chattering meanwhile in a language we could not understand, and clutching at ropes and gangways, they swarmed up the ship's side with such speed and _____ that they almost seemed to fly." *The Arabian Nights* by Andrew Lang

4. "She is not rich; she has only an _____ of twelve hundred francs, and it would be impossible for her to send me to school." *The Professor* by Charlotte Bronte

5. "As he finished the _____ the Thing shuddered throughout its huge bulk, the Gump gave the screeching cry that is familiar to those animals, and then the four wings began flopping furiously." *The Marvelous Land of Oz* by L. Frank Baum

6. "Therefore Marilla conceived it to be her duty to drill Anne into a tranquil uniformity of disposition as impossible and _____ to her as to a dancing sunbeam in one of the brook shallows." *Anne of Green Gables* by Lucy Maud Montgomery

7. "Neither could he mobilize his army to go forth to war, nor could he punish his _____ subjects." *The Iron Heel* by Jack London

8. "The little pink sloth-creature was still blinking at me when my Ape-man reappeared at the _____ of the nearest of these dens, and beckoned me in." *The Island Doctor* by H.G. Wells

9. "Such shock was productive of molecular changes in the _____ cells." *Before Adam* by Jack London

10. "Wilfred Bohun stood rooted to the spot long enough to see the idiot go out into the sunshine, and even to see his dissolute brother hail him with a sort of _____ jocularity." *The Innocence of Father Brown* by Gilbert K. Chesterton

Quiz 2: Chapters 6-10

Censor, Accessory, Incite, Century, Acclaim
Cloister, Complement, Incognito, Corpse, Creed

1. "But the ship, having her full _____ of seamen, spurned his suit; and not all the King his father's influence could prevail." *Moby Dick* by Herman Melville

2. "I have come _____ from Prague for the purpose of consulting you." *The Adventures of Sherlock Holmes* by Sir Arthur Conan Doyle

3. "The master's wife called him the "Blessed Wolf," which name was taken up with _____ and all the women called him the Blessed Wolf." *White Fang* by Jack London

4. "This was the _____ of the nuns, and the old woman was the Abbess." *The Yellow Fairy Book* by Andrew Lang

5. "Or is there a pleasure in being _____ to a theft when we cannot commit it ourselves?" *The History of Tom Jones* by Henry Fielding

6. "He is a great teacher, a corrector of morals, a _____ of vice, and a commender of virtue." *Fables* by Aesop

7. "Was this genuine, he wondered, a voluntary outburst, or was it some subtle attempt to _____ sympathy?" *The Vanished Messenger* by E. Phillips Oppenheim

8. "The adventures of the Yellow Diamond begin with the eleventh _____ of the Christian era." *The Moonstone* by Wilkie Collins

9. "Doubtless, and we are not now inquiring into his _____, but his actions; in the name of the prefect of police, I ask you what you know of him." *The Count of Monte Cristo* by Alexandre Dumas

10. "The _____ was dressed in a uniform that once had been blue, but was now faded to a mel-ancholy shade of green." *The Red Badge of Courage* by Stephen Crane

Quiz 3: Chapters 11-15

Concur, Docile, Diction, Domestic, Erroneous
Endorse, Deface, Infallible, Fidelity, Affinity

1. "Not with the organs of sight; but with much more _____ instruments of vision: the conclusions of reason, and the deductions of scientific premises." *The Prairie* by James Fenimore Cooper

2. "Now old man, let us 'pud' along; it's getting late for the chicken," he added, relapsing into the graceful _____ with which a classical education gifts its fortunate possessor." *An Old-Fashioned Girl* by Louisa May Alcott

3. "This order of truth, no matter how _____ it may be, is the sane and normal order of the truth, the rational order." *John Barleycorn* by Jack London

4. "It was the soft, amiable Negro voice, like those I remember from early childhood, with the note of _____ subservience in it." *My Antonia* by Willa Cather

5. "I embrace this opportunity to assure you once more of my unalterable _____ to your interests." *No Name* by Wilke Collins

6. "And bringing in her brother Stevie as soon as she could into the current of _____ events, she mentioned that the boy had moped a good deal." *The Secret Agent* by Joseph Conrad

7. "I am obliged to you for your good opinion, 'retorted the single gentlemen,' and quite _____ in these sentiments." *The Old Curiosity Shop* by Charles Dickens

8. "SIR,--I have duly received your note, in which you claim to _____ my views, although I am not aware that they are dependent upon endorsement either from you or anyone else." *The Lost World* by Sir Arthur Conan Doyle

9. "Fortunately, nothing can _____ the beauty of a ship." *The Mirror of the Sea* by Joseph Conrad"

10. Caustic potash has a great _____ for carbonic acid; and it is sufficient to shake it in order for it to seize upon the acid and form bicarbonate of potassium."   *From The Earth To The Moon* by Jules Verne

Quiz 4: Chapters 16-20

Inflection, Deflect, Fugitive, Fragile, Diffuse
Gorge, Congregation, Gradual, Itinerary, Inherent

1. "In another moment we were standing face to face, I and this _____ thing out of futurity." *The Time Machine* by H.G. Wells

2. "The _____ being fully assembled, how, the bell rang once more, to warn laggards and stragglers, and then a solemn hush fell upon the church." *Tom Sawyer* by Mark Twain

3. "Yet suicide, quick or slow, a sudden spill or a _____ oozing away through the years, is the price John Barleycorn exacts." *John Barleycorn* by Jack London

4. "This plan, which he brought to the comte, was a map of France, upon which the practiced eye of that gentleman discovered an _____, marked out with small pins; wherever a pin was missing, a hole denoted it's having been there." *The Man in the Iron Mask* by Alexandre Dumas

5. "The vapour did not _____ as a true gas would do." *The War Of The Worlds* by H.G. Wells

6. "The afternoon had been dull and cloudy and now as he was passing through a narrow _____ a few great drops of rain began to splatter upon his naked shoulders." *Tarzan the Untamed* by Edgar Rice Burroughs

7. "There was a rising _____ in her voice." *Pollyanna* by Eleanor H. Porter

8. "Just at the door the captain aimed at the _____ one last tremendous cut, which would certainly have split him to the chine had it not been intercepted by our big signboard of Admiral Benbow." *Treasure Island* by Robert Louis Stevenson

9. "Biographical historians and historians of separate nations understand this force as a power _____ in heroes and rulers." *War and Peace* by Leo Tolstoy

10. "Quick as had been the flash of the long handled tomahawk, he had been quick enough to duck away his head and partially to _____ the stroke with this up-flung hand." *The Red One* by Jack London

Quiz 5: Chapters 21-27

Projectile, Jocular, Deluge, Levity, License
Literal, Mediocre, Colloquial, Immersion, Missile

1. "Her husband's quiet tastes irritate her, I think, and she finds it worth while to play the patroness to a group of young poets and painters of advanced ideas and _____ ability." *My Antonia* by Willa Cather

2. "Again he pressed the hand of the latter with an expression of good-natured, sincere, and animated _____. *War and Peace* by Leo Tolstoy

3. "As in droughty regions baptism by _____ could only be performed symbolically." *Middlemarch* by George Eliot

4. "That night another invisible _____ started on its way to the earth from Mars, just a second or so under twenty-four hours after the first one." *The War Of The Worlds* by H.G. Wells

5. "Strangely enough, in both cases I took to that sort of thing in circumstances in which I did not expect, in _____ phrase, 'to come out of it.'" *The Shadow Line* by Joseph Conrad

6. "Here is the _____ copy of it, word for word…" *The Moonstone* by Wilkie Collins

7. "The water-colour lesson enlivened by the _____ conversation of the kindly, humorous, old man was always great fun; and she felt she would be compensated for the tiresome beginning of the day." *Chance* by Joseph Conrad

8. "A few years since the annual charge for a cab _____ was very much reduced, and the difference between the six and seven days' cabs was abolished." *Black Beauty* by Anna Sewell

9. "He recovered himself amidst a _____ of interrogations." *The Man in the Iron Mask* by Alexandre Dumas

10. "An enormous hole had been made by the impact of the _____, and the sand and gravel had been flung violently in every direction over the heath, forming heaps visible a mile and a half away." *The War Of The Worlds* by H.G. Wells

Answer Key

Lesson I

Exercise A
1. acrid. 2. exacerbate. 3. alias. 4. agility. 5. acerbity. 6. altitude. 7. alteration. 8. acrimonious. 9. acute. 10. agitate. 11. altruistic. 12. acuity. 13. agrarian. 14. alienate. 15. acumen. 16. alter. 17. aliens. 18. alternated. 19. altimeter. 20. agriculture.

Exercise B
1. r. 2. g. 3. i. 4. l. 5. o. 6. c. 7. j. 8. a. 9. b. 10. q. 11. h. 12. e. 13. s. 14. f. 15. d. 16. n. 17. k. 18. t. 19. p. 20. m.

Lesson II

Exercise A
1. amicable. 2. annual. 3. equanimity. 4. animadversion. 5. inept. 6. perennial. 7. ambulatory. 8. animosity. 9. perambulator. 10. aperture. 11. amorous. 12. enamored. 13. animate. 14. unanimous. 15. annuity. 16. amateur. 17. somnambulate. 18. aptitude. 19. amiable. 20. amity.

Exercise B
1. k. 2. a. 3. h. 4. c. 5. f. 6. p. 7. s. 8. e. 9. n. 10. b. 11. k. 12. m. 13. o. 14. l. 15. q. 16. d. 17. t. 18. i. 19. g. 20. r.

Lesson III

Exercise A
1. disarmament. 2. artisans. 3. artless. 4. battery. 5. audible. 6. beatitude. 7. army. 8. audience. 9. battlement. 10. beatific. 11. artifice. 12. auditorium. 13. abate. 14. debase. 15. artifact. 16. avuncular. 17. aureate. 18. aureole. 19. artificial. 20. audial.

Exercise B
1. k. 2. g. 3. q. 4. j. 5. t. 6. r. 7. n. 8. s. 9. o. 10. f. 11. l. 12. a. 13. d. 14. p. 15. b. 16. h. 17. i. 18. c. 19. e. 20. m.

Lesson IV

Exercise A
1. casualty. 2. abbreviation. 3. antebellum. 4. decadent. 5. imbibe. 6. recalcitrant. 7. candid. 8. deciduous. 9. rebellious. 10. recant. 11. abbreviations. 12. candor. 13. cascades. 14. brevity. 15. Incandescent. 16. belligerent or bellicose. 17. candidate. 18. cadence. 19. incantation. 20. bellicose or belligerent.

Exercise B
1. o. 2. f. 3. c. 4. m 5. l. 6. d. 7. e. 8. h. 9. t. 10. p. 11. s. 12. i. 13. a. 14. k. 15. b. 16. n. 17. j. 18. q. 19. g. 20. r.

Lesson V

Exercise A
1. decapitate. 2. deception. 3. inception. 4. recapitulate. 5. capture. 6. castigate. 7. carnivorous. 8. carnal. 9. discreet. 10. participated. 11. carnage. 12. incarnate. 13. recipient. 14. ascertain. 15. cerebral. 16. cerebration. 17. chasten. 18. discretion. 19. certitude. 20. participation.
Exercise B
1. t. 2. h. 3. g. 4. l. 5. d. 6. p. 7. f. 8. r. 9. e. 10. o. 11. i. 12. c. 13. k. 14. j. 15. m. 16. n. 17. q. 18. s. 19. b. 20. a.

Lesson VI

Exercise A
1. access. 2. proceeded. 3. census. 4. precedes. 5. accessories. 6. accede. 7. censorious. 8. decelerate. 9. cede. 10. accession. 11. censure. 12. receded. 13. concessions. 14. procession. 15. concede. 16. censor. 17. accelerate. 18. celerity. 19. recession.
Exercise B
1. n. 2. m. 3. g. 4. p. 5. a. 6. j. 7. l. 8. b. 9. o. 10. r. 11. q. 12. c. 13. s. 14. k. 15. d. 16. e. 17. h. 18. i. 19. f.

Lesson VII

Exercise A
1. centenary or centennial. 2. incision. 3. century. 4. excite. 5. suicide. 6. centipede. 7. civilian. 8. concise. 9. recitation. 10. centennial or centenary. 11. civilization. 12. incited. 13. herbicide. 14. centigrade. 15. homicide. 16. civil. 17. bicentennial. 18. recite. 19. precise. 20. incise.
Exercise B
1. b. 2. e. 3. n. 4. q. 5. h. 6. f. 7. m. 8. o. 9. t. 10. c. 11. r. 12. d. 13. k. 14. a. 15. j. 16. p. 17. l. 18. g. 19. i. 20. s.

Lesson VIII

Exercise A
1. clarify. 2. acclamation. 3. clarity. 4. occlude. 5. enclave. 6. clamorous. 7. reclusion. 8. cloister. 9. declaimed. 10. recluse. 11. clavier. 12. claustrophobia. 13. enclose. 14. declamation. 15. acclaim. 16. clarion. 17. clavicle. 18. closure. 19. enclosure. 20. clamor.
Exercise B
1. n. 2. j. 3. p. 4. h. 5. g. 6. s. 7. d. 8. m. 9. q. 10. b. 11. e. 12. o. 13. a. 14. i. 15. t. 16. l. 17. r. 18. c. 19. f. 20. k.

Test 1

ANSWER KEY

1. acerbity	a. bitterness
2. acumen	c. insight
3. acute	e. intense
4. altruistic	d. selfless
5. exacerbate	b. aggravate
6. amicable	c. friendly
7. aptitude	d. ability
8. perennial	c. enduring
9. abate	a. decrease
10. aureate	c. golden
11. avuncular	d. like an uncle
12. bellicose	a. hostile
13. cadence	b. rhythmic flow
14. imbibe	c. drink
15. recalcitrant	d. resistant
16. carnal	b. sexual
17. castigates	a. criticizes
18. discreet	e. circumspect
19. recapitulate	d. summarize
20. celerity	c. haste
21. censure	b. criticism
22. precede	a. go before
23. precise	c. exact
24. clarion	b. trumpet
25. cloister	c. place for religious seclusion

Lesson IX

Exercise A
1. complement. 2. accolade. 3. cognizant. 4. accord. 5. inclination. 6. inclined. 7. declivity. 8. cognition. 9. incognito. 10. decline. 11. complementary. 12. cordial. 13. reclined. 14. concoct. 15. proclivity (or inclination). 16. concordance. 17. concord. 18. precocious. 19. comply. 20. copious.

Exercise B
1. c. 2. g. 3. m. 4. a. 5. s. 6. j. 7. r. 8. e. 9. l. 10. o. 11. p. 12. d. 13. n. 14. q. 15. i. 16. h. 17. b. 18. k. 19. f. 20. t.

Lesson X

Exercise A
1. corpulent. 2. incorporate. 3. corporal. 4. creed. 5. accrue. 6. credulity. 7. inculpate. 8. corpses. 9. creditable. 10. succumb. 11. culpable. 12. recumbent. 13. cruciform. 14. covet. 15. crescendo. 16. excrescence. 17. incubus. 18. cupidity. 19. accumulate. 20. incumbent.

Exercise B
1. l. 2. s. 3. e. 4. i. 5. b. 6. q. 7. g. 8. k. 9. c. 10. h. 11. a. 12. r. 13. p. 14. f. 15. m. 16. o. 17. n. 18. t. 19. j. 20. d.

Lesson XI

Exercise A
1. trident. 2. excursion. 3. docile. 4. incur. 5. mandate. 6. cursory. 7. ambidextrous. 8. succor. 9. curriculum. 10. precursor . 11. data. 12. discourse. 13. concur. 14. deities. 15. deify. 16. indentation. 17. divinity. 18. concurrent. 19. divine. 20. incursion .

Exercise B
1. p. 2. j. 3. r. 4. e. 5. g. 6. q. 7. a. 8. n. 9. s. 10. h. 11. d. 12. c. 13. l. 14. k. 15. t. 16. m. 17. b. 18. o. 19. i. 20. f.

Lesson XII

Exercise A
1. domestic. 2. dictum. 3. jurisdiction. 4. domain. 5. dominant. 6. diction. 7. interdiction. 8. domineer. 9. verdict. 10. dominate. 11. edict. 12. malediction. 13. dictator. 14. domicile. 15. valediction. 16. ditty. 17. condolence. 18. benediction. 19. dominion. 20. condoled.

Exercise B
1. t. 2. f. 3. s. 4. r. 5. h. 6. n. 7. b. 8. l. 9. e. 10. a. 11. i. 12. q. 13. c. 14. m. 15. d. 16. j. 17. g. 18. o. 19. p. 20. k.

Lesson XIII

Exercise A
1. indomitable. 2. egocentric. 3. equal. 4. equity. 5. dorsal. 6. endorsed. 7. deduce. 8. traduce. 9. error. 10. daunt. 11. aberration. 12. dormant. 13. induce. 14. viaducts. 15. errant. 16. erratic. 17. erroneous. 18. egotists. 19. aqueducts. 20. dauntless.

Exercise B
1. t. 2. n. 3. b. 4. f. 5. m. 6. g. 7. e. 8. j. 9. l. 10. p. 11. q. 12. a. 13. h. 14. o. 15. r. 16. d. 17. k. 18. i. 19. s. 20. c.

Lesson XIV

Exercise A
1. deface. 2. infallible. 3. fervent. 4. façade. 5. affable. 6. mollify. 7. effervescent. 8. facet. 9. affect. 10. fallacious. 11. rectify. 12. fiction. 13. fervor. 14. facile. 15. falsify. 16. facsimile. 17. ineffable. 18. fetish. 19. effacing. 20. fallacy.

Exercise B
1. m. 2. g. 3. r. 4. i. 5. s. 6. c. 7. l. 8. e. 9. k. 10. f. 11. t. 12. a. 13. j. 14. o. 15. b. 16. q. 17. d. 18. h. 19. p. 20. n.

Test 2

1. cordial	d. gracious
2. copious	c. plentiful
3. incognito	a. disguised
4. proclivity	d. tendency
5. precocious	b. mature

6. credulity	e. tendency to believe
7. culpable	b. guilty
8. incumbent	a. obligatory
9. cursory	c. superficial
10. docile	a. obedient
11. condole	b. express sorrow
12. diction	d. enunciation
13. dominion	c. sovereignty
14. verdict	e. decision of a jury
15. daunt	c. dismay
16. dorsal	b. on the back
17. endorse	a. approve
18. errant	c. wandering
19. viaduct	b. bridge
20. affable	d. friendly
21. affect	c. influence
22. façade	b. exterior
23. facsimile	e. copy
24. fetish	d. idol
25. mollify	c. appease

Lesson XV

Exercise A
1. transfer. 2. affinity. 3. elation. 4. refer. 5. translate. 6. defer. 7. definitive. 8. dilatory. 9. inferred. 10. infidel. 11. confer. 12. finite. 13. festoon. 14. confine. 15. festive. 16. confidence. 17. fidelity. 18. define. 19. conifers. 20. fertile.

Exercise B
1. l. 2. f. 3. n. 4. h. 5. s. 6. k. 7. i. 8. j. 9. c. 10. r. 11. m. 12. g. 13. e. 14. o. 15. p. 16. d. 17. b. 18. t. 19. q. 20. a.

Lesson XVI

Exercise A
1. infirm. 2. influx. 3. figurative. 4. fluctuate. 5. deflect. 6. fluent. 7. configuration. 8. inflection. 9. floral. 10. effluent. 11. confirm. 12. florid. 13. flux. 14. flora. 15. fluid. 16. confirm. 17. infirmary. 18. genuflect. 19. confluent. 20. affluent.

Exercise B
1. q. 2. o. 3. l. 4. h. 5. n. 6. g. 7. s. 8. c. 9. e. 10. a. 11. m. 12. b. 13. f. 14. p. 15. d. 16. r. 17. k. 18. t. 19. j. 20. i.

Lesson XVII

Exercise A
1. refractory. 2. fragile. 3. forum. 4. affront. 5. fraternizing. 6. fracture. 7. infraction. 8. fugitive. 9. fortuitous. 10. frail. 11. fortunate. 12. refuge. 13. forensic. 14. fraternal. 15. infringe. 16. fragments. 17. fortified. 18. confront. 19. fratricide. 20. fortitude.

Exercise B
1. r. 2. d. 3. e. 4. t. 5. b. 6. a. 7. n.. 8. h. 9. i. 10. p. 11. m. 12. g. 13. k. 14. c. 15. q. 16. l. 17. j. 18. s. 19. o. 20. f.

Lesson XVIII

Exercise A
1. progenitor. 2. engender. 3. gentile. 4. congenital 5. ingenuous. 6. fusion. 7. gorge. 8. transfuse. 9. profuse. 10. genre. 11. gentry. 12. generous. 13. diffuse. 14. genuine. 15. generate. 16. genteel. 17. effusive. 18. regenerate. 19. regurgitate. 20. genus.
Exercise B
1. p. 2. n. 3. f. 4. e. 5. k. 6. c. 7. l. 8. o. 9. g. 10. t. 11. j. 12. r. 13. s. 14. m. 15. b. 16. q. 17. d. 18. h. 19. a. 20. i. 21. u

Lesson XIX

Exercise A
1. aggregate. 2. congregations. 3. gradient. 4. gradual. 5. degraded. 6. digress. 7. gratified. 8. ingredient. 9. transgressed. 10. segregation. 11. gratitude. 12. gregarious. 13. retrograde. 14. egregious. 15. progress. 16. conglomerate. 17. congratulations. 18. regress. 19. grateful. 20. graduate.
Exercise B
1. i.. 2. b. 3. g. 4. f. 5. q. 6. t. 7. h. 8. s. 9. a. 10. l. 11. r. 12. j. 13. c. 14. m. 15. p. 16. k. 17. n. 18. e. 19. d. 20. o.

Lesson XX

Exercise A
1. circuit. 2. cohesion. 3. itinerary. 4. expletive. 5. irascible. 6. inherent. 7. adhesion. 8. incense. 9. deplete. 10. transition. 11. adhere. 12. itinerant. 13. incoherent. 14. implement. 15. coherent. 16. circuitous. 17. incendiary. 18. irate. 19. replete. 20. adhesive. 21. transitory. 22. transit.
Exercise B
1. j. 2. r. 3. p. 4. l. 5. k. 6. f. 7. o. 8. a. 9. c. 10. s. 11. d. 12. b. 13. q. 14. e. 15. n. 16. h. 17. i. 18. g. 19. t. 20. m. 21. u. 22. v

Test 3

1. affinity   b. natural sympathy
2. confer   a. bestow
3. infer   a. deduce
4. finite   c. limited
5. affirm   b. declare to be true
6. affluent   d. generously supplied, rich
7. flora   c. plants
8. fortuitous   d. accidental
9. forensic   b. relating to evidence

ANSWER KEY

10. fusion	b. merging
11. genre	a. category
12. gentry	c. upper class
13. gorge	d. ravine
14. progenitor	e. father
15. aggregate	a. collective whole
16. conglomerate	c. clustered
17. egregious	b. outstandingly bad
18. gradient	b. slope
19. gregarious	d. social
20. adhere	c. stick fast
21. expletive	b. exclamatory
22. irascible	d. easily angered
23. itinerant	c. traveling
24. incendiary	a. flammable
25. replete	d. abundant

Lesson XXI

Exercise A
1. jocular. 2. trajectory. 3. prejudice. 4. abject. 5. adjunct. 6. perjured. 7. subjunctive. 8. inject. 9. conjunction. 10. conjecture. 11. projectile. 12. conjure. 13. jury. 14. judicious. 15. junction. 16. interjection. 17. conjugal. 18. adjudicate. 19. ejaculatory. 20. abjure. 21. juncture.

Exercise B
1. l. 2. q. 3. b. 4. h. 5. d. 6. r. 7. j. 8. n. 9. c. 10. s. 11. a. 12. o. 13. p. 14. u. 15. f. 16. t. 17. k. 18. e. 19. i. 20. m. 21. g.

Lesson XXII

Exercise A
1. leverage. 2. allege. 3. equilateral. 4. legitimate. 5. elevated. 6. legate. 7. levity. 8. collaborate. 9. laborious. 10. legal. 11. alleviate. 12. ablutions. 13. legacy. 14. collateral. 15. deluge. 16. relegate. 17. allegation. 18. legislature. 19. litigate. 20. levitation.

Exercise B
1. j. 2. a. 3. i. 4. m. 5. b. 6. q. 7. n. 8. k. 9. o. 10. s. 11. l. 12. c. 13. p. 14. t. 15. f. 16. h. 17. r. 18. g. 19. e. 20. d.

Lesson XXIII

Exercise A
1. league. 2. licentious. 3. locality. 4. libertine. 5. liberty. 6. libretto. 7. linguistics. 8. ligation. 9. liberation. 10. illicit. 11. locus. 12. libel. 13. license. 14. alliteration. 15. ligature. 16. lingual. 17. locales. 18. liberal. 19. obliterate. 20. literal.

Exercise B
1. t. 2. h. 3. e. 4. j. 5. p. 6. b. 7. r. 8. l. 9. f. 10. c. 11. n. 12. d. 13. m. 14. q. 15. g. 16. i. 17. k. 18. s. 19. o. 20. a.

Lesson XXIV

Exercise A

1. delusion. 2. elude. 3. allusion. 4. luminescence. 5. obloquy. 6. colloquial. 7. illuminate. 8. lucid. 9. Loquacious. 10. luminous. 11. elucidate. 12. collusion. 13. elocution. 14. alluded. 15. luminary. 16. soliloquy. 17. lucent. 18. eloquent. 19. pellucid. 20. elusive.

Exercise B

1. h. 2. m. 3. p. 4. s. 5. n. 6. o. 7. c. 8. j. 9. r. 10. g. 11. e. 12. a. 13. q. 14. d. 15. k. 16. t. 17. i. 18. l. 19. f. 20. b.

Lesson XXV

Exercise A

1. matriculate. 2. manuscript. 3. mediocre. 4. mariner. 5. maternity. 6. emancipate. 7. matriarch. 8. manipulated. 9. mediate. 10. mandatory. 11. marinade. 12. manufacture. 13. cormorant. 14. maritime. 15. mandate. 16. maternal. 17. medieval. 18. manifest. 19. matrix. 20. matrimony. 21. submarine.

Exercise B

1. c. 2. i. 3. m. 4. f. 5. k. 6. e. 7. n. 8. s. 9. o. 10. h. 11. b. 12. q. 13. d. 14. j. 15. a. 16. r. 17. t. 18. l. 19. p. 20. g. 21. u.

Lesson XXVI

Exercise A

1. memorandum. 2. emerge. 3. minutia. 4. mendacious. 5. minister. 6. immemorial. 7. minimize. 8. meritorious. 9. memorabilia. 10. merge. 11. emendations. 12. reminiscent. 13. mellifluous. 14. memoir. 15. immersion. 16. mendicant. 17. meretricious. 18. memory. 19. minimal. 20. minute. 21. submerged. 22. mend.

Exercise B

1. i. 2. m. 3. e. 4. n. 5. q. 6. s. 7. t. 8. k. 9. a. 10. u. 11. p. 12. l. 13. b. 14. h. 15. f. 16. r. 17. d. 18. o. 19. j. 20. c. 21. g. 22. v.

Lesson XXVII

Exercise A

1. motion. 2. commit. 3. premise. 4. submit. 5. missile. 6. demise. 7. remit. 8. permissive. 9. admitted. 10. immovable. 11. momentum. 12. moment. 13. permit. 14. missive. 15. admittance. 16. emissary. 17. transmit. 18. mobilize. 19. remote. 20. emit. 21. permission. 22. emission. 23. promise.

Exercise B

1. k. 2. c. 3. h. 4. n. 5. l. 6. d. 7. q. 8. g. 9. i. 10. a. 11. e. 12. s. 13. f. 14. m. 15. o. 16. p. 17. b. 18. t. 19. r. 20. j. 21. u. 22. w. 23. v.

Test 4

1. abject — b. hopeless
2. abjure — c. forswear
3. adjunct — a. joined but subordinate
4. jocular — e. joking
5. ablution — d. washing
6. legate — c. official emissary
7. elevate — b. promote
8. alleviate — e. ease
9. inherent — a. intrinsic
10. alliteration — d. repetition of a sound at the beginning of words
11. libel — c. false disparagement
12. libertine — a. philanderer
13. licentious — b. promiscuous
14. obliterate — e. erase
15. colloquial — b. conversational
16. eloquent — c. expressive
17. elude — a. evade
18. emancipate — c. liberate
19. manifest — d. demonstrate
20. Matriarch — a. female head of family
21. medieval — c. belonging to the Middle Ages
22. mendicant — b. beggar
23. meritorious — d. praiseworthy
24. emissary — e. agent
25. missive — c. letter

Quiz 1

1. Artificial
2. Carnivorous
3. Agility
4. Annuity
5. Incantation
6. Alien
7. Recalcitrant
8. Aperture
9. Cerebral
10. Avuncular

Quiz 2

1. Complement
2. Incognito
3. Acclaim
4. Cloister
5. Accessory
6. Censor
7. Incite
8. Century
9. Creed
10. Corpse

Quiz 3

1. Infallible
2. Diction
3. Erroneous
4. Docile
5. Fidelity
6. Domestic
7. Concur
8. Endorse
9. Deface
10. Affinity

Quiz 4

1. Fragile
2. Congregation
3. Gradual
4. Itinerary
5. Diffuse
6. Gorge
7. Inflection
8. Fugitive
9. Inherent
10. Deflect

Quiz 5

1. Mediocre
2. Levity
3. Immersion
4. Missile
5. Colloquial
6. Literal
7. Jocular
8. License
9. Deluge
10. Projectile

Index

abate..................20
abbreviate............26
abbreviation.........26
aberration.............85
abject..................140
abjure.................142
ablution..............147
accede.................37
accelerate............38
access.................40
accession............37
accessory............37
acclaim...............49
acclamation.........49
accolade..............60
accord.................61
accrue.................66
accumulate..........66
acerbity................7
acrid.....................7
acrimonious..........7
acuity...................7
acumen................7
acute....................8
adhere................129
adhesion............129
adhesive............129
adjudicate..........141
adjunct..............141
admit..................176
admittance.........176
affable................91
affect..................89
affinity...............100
affirm.................105
affluent..............106
affront...............113
aggregate..........125

agility..................8
agitate..................8
agrarian...............8
agriculture...........8
alias.....................8
alien....................8
alienate...............8
allegation..........147
allege................147
alleviate.............148
alliteration.........154
allude................159
allusion..............160
alter....................8
alteration.............9
alternate..............9
altimeter..............9
altitude................9
altruistic..............9
amateur..............13
ambidextrous......72
ambulatory.........14
amiable..............13
amicable............13
amity.................13
amorous.............13
animadversion....13
animate..............13
animosity...........13
annual................13
annuity..............14
antebellum.........25
aperture.............15
aptitude.............15
aqueduct............84
army..................19
artifact...............19
artifice...............19

artificial.............19
artisan................20
artless................20
ascertain............33
audial.................20
audible..............20
audience............20
auditorium........20
aureate..............20
aureole..............20
avuncular..........20
battery..............20
battlement.........21
beatific..............21
beatitude...........21
bellicose............25
belligerent.........25
benediction.......77
bicentennial......43
brevity..............26
cadence............26
candid..............26
candidate.........26
candor.............27
capture.............31
carnage.............32
carnal...............32
carnivorous......32
cascade.............26
castigate............32
casualty............26
cede..................37
celerity..............38
censor...............38
censorious........39
censure.............39
census..............39
centenary.........43

205

centennial............43	confidence...........100	definitive............101
centigrade............43	configuration......105	deflect.................106
centipede.............43	confine................101	degrade................123
century.................43	confirm................105	deify.....................72
cerebral................32	confluent.............106	deity......................72
cerebration...........32	confront...............113	deluge..................147
certitude...............33	congenital............118	delusion...............160
chasten..................32	conglomerate.....123	demise.................176
circuit.................131	congratulation....124	deplete................130
circuitous...........131	congregation......125	dictator.................77
civil......................44	conifer..................99	diction..................77
civilian.................44	conjecture...........140	dictum..................77
civilization...........45	conjugal..............141	diffuse.................117
clamor..................49	conjunction........141	digress.................123
clamorous.............49	copious.................60	dilatory.................99
clarify...................50	cordial..................61	disarmament........19
clarion..................50	corporal................65	discourse..............72
clarity...................50	corpse...................65	discreet.................33
claustrophobia......51	corpulent..............65	discretion.............33
clavicle.................51	covet.....................67	ditty......................77
clavier..................51	credible................65	divine...................73
cloister.................50	creditable.............65	divinity.................73
closure..................50	credulity...............66	docile....................73
cognition..............60	crescendo.............66	domain.................78
cognizance...........60	cruciform.............66	domestic...............78
coherent.............129	culpable................66	domicile................78
cohesion............129	cupidity................67	dominant..............78
collaborate.........146	curriculum...........71	dominate..............79
collateral...........146	cursory.................71	domineer..............79
colloquial...........158	data......................72	dominion..............79
collusion............160	daunt....................83	dormant................83
commit...............176	dauntless..............83	dorsal....................84
complement.........60	debase..................20	edict......................78
complementary....60	decadent..............26	efface....................90
comply.................60	decapitate.............32	effervescent..........91
concede................38	decelerate.............38	effluent...............106
concession............38	deception..............31	effusive...............117
concise.................44	deciduous.............26	egocentric.............84
concoct.................60	declaim.................49	egotist...................84
concord................61	declamation.........49	egregious............125
concordance.........61	decline..................59	ejaculatory.........140
concur..................71	declivity...............59	elation..................99
concurrent...........71	deduce..................84	elevate................148
condole................78	deface..................90	elocution............158
condolence...........78	defer......................99	eloquent.............158
confer...................99	define..................101	elucidate.............159

INDEX

elude..................160
elusive................130
emancipate.........164
emendation........171
emerge...............171
emissary.............176
emission.............177
emit....................177
enamored............14
enclave................51
enclose................50
enclosure.............50
endorse................84
engender............118
equal....................84
equanimity..........14
equilateral.........147
equity..................85
errant...................85
erratic..................85
erroneous............85
error....................85
exacerbate............8
excite..................44
excrescence.........66
excursion.............72
expletive............130
façade..................90
facet....................90
facile...................89
facsimile..............89
fallacious.............90
fallacy.................90
falsify..................90
façade..................90
fertile.................100
fervent.................91
fervor...................91
festoon...............100
fetish...................89
fiction..................90
fidelity...............100
figurative..........105
finite..................101
flora..................106
floral.................106

florid..................106
fluctuate............107
fluent.................107
fluid...................107
flux....................107
forensic..............111
fortify................111
fortitude............111
fortuitous...........111
fortunate...........111
forum................112
fracture.............112
fragile................112
fragment...........112
frail...................112
fraternal............112
fraternize..........112
fratricide...........113
fugitive..............113
fusion................117
generate............118
generous...........118
genre.................118
genteel..............118
gentile...............118
gentry...............118
genuflect...........106
genuine.............119
genus................119
gorge.................118
gradient............124
gradual.............124
graduate...........124
grateful.............125
gratify...............125
gratitude...........125
gregarious.........125
herbicide............44
homicide............44
illicit..................153
illuminate.........159
imbibe................26
immemorial.....170
immersion........172
immovable.......178
implement........130

incandescent........27
incantation...........27
incarnate..............32
incendiary..........130
incense...............130
inception..............32
incise...................44
incision................44
incite...................44
inclination...........59
inclined...............59
incognito.............60
incoherent.........130
incorporate.........65
incubus................66
inculpate.............67
incumbent..........66
incur...................72
incursion.............72
indentation.........72
indomitable........83
induce.................84
ineffable.............91
inept...................15
infallible.............90
infer..................100
infidel...............100
infirm................106
infirmary..........106
inflection..........106
influx................107
infraction.........112
infringe............112
ingenuous.........119
ingredient.........124
inherent............130
inject.................140
interdiction........78
interjection......141
irascible............130
irate..................130
itinerant...........131
itinerary...........131
jocular..............141
judicious..........141
juncture...........141

207

jurisdiction............78	matriarch.............165	proceed................38
laborious............146	matriculate.........165	procession............38
league.................153	matrimony..........166	proclivity..............60
legacy.................147	matrix..................166	profuse...............117
legal....................147	mediate................166	progenitor...........119
legate..................148	medieval..............166	progress..............124
legislature..........147	mediocre..............166	projectile............141
legitimate...........147	mellifluous..........170	rebellious.............25
leverage..............148	memoir................170	recalcitrant..........26
levitation............148	memorabilia........170	recant..................26
levity..................148	memorandum.....171	recapitulate...........32
libel....................152	memory...............171	recede..................38
liberal.................152	mend...................171	recession..............38
liberation............152	mendacious.........171	recipient..............32
libertine..............153	mendicant............171	recitation..............44
liberty.................153	meretricious........171	recite....................44
libretto................152	merge..................172	recline..................59
license................153	meritorious..........171	recluse..................50
licentious............153	minimal...............172	reclusion...............50
ligation...............153	minimize.............172	rectify...................90
ligature...............153	minister...............172	recumbent............66
lingual.................153	minute.................172	refer....................100
linguistic.............153	minutia................172	refractory............112
literal..................154	missile.................177	refuge..................113
litigate................147	missive................177	regenerate...........119
locality...............154	mobilize..............178	regress.................124
locus...................154	mollify..................90	regurgitate..........118
loquacious..........158	moment...............178	relegate...............148
lucent.................159	momentum..........178	reminiscent........171
lucid...................159	motion.................178	remit...................177
luminary.............159	obliterate............154	remote.................178
luminescence.....159	obloquy...............158	replete.................130
luminous............159	occlude.................50	retrograde...........124
malediction...........78	participate............31	segregation.........125
mandate................72	participation.........31	soliloquy............159
mandate..............164	pellucid...............159	somnambulate......14
mandatory..........164	perennial...............15	subjunctive.........142
manifest..............164	perjure................142	submarine..........165
manipulate..........164	permissive...........177	submit................177
manufacture.......165	permit.................177	succor...................72
manuscript..........165	precede.................38	succumb...............66
marinade.............165	precise..................44	suicide..................44
mariner...............165	precocious............60	traduce................84
maritime.............165	precursor..............72	trajectory............141
maternal.............165	prejudice............141	transfer...............100
maternity............165	premise...............177	transfuse.............117

transgress............124
transit..................131
transition.............131
transitory.............131

translate...............100
transmit...............177
trident....................72
unanimous............14

valediction............78
verdict...................78
viaduct..................84

www.ingramcontent.com/pod-product-compliance
Lightning Source LLC
Chambersburg PA
CBHW060313240426
43661CB00059B/2752